Overcoming Job Burnout

How to Renew Enthusiasm for Work

Dr. Beverly Potter

"docpotter"

Ronin Publishing

Berkeley, CA

www.roninpub.com

Here's what they say about *Overcoming Job Burnout*

"Remarkably insightful and exciting...offers wise, powerful, useful advice on many levels—good medicine indeed."—*Miami Herald*

"Dr. Potter's surefire burnout remedy...explains how to succeed in corporate life while 'keeping your souls alive.' "—*Berkeley Voice*

"Guidelines to help you keep your emotional health *and* your job." —*Redbook Magazine*

"Self-discovery, goal-setting, planning and dreaming is time well spent."—*Glamour*

"Potter's remedy for writer burnout."
—*Writer's Digest*

"Worthwhile reading."
—Executive Female

"Tells the individual what he can do for himself."—*San Francisco Chronicle*

"If it's possible to cure job burnout with a book, this one could do it."—*Savvy Magazine*

Overcoming Job Burnout

How to Renew Enthusiasm for Work

OVERCOMING JOB BURNOUT, Third Edition

ISBN: 1-57951-074-4

Copyright © 1980, 1985, 1993, 1998, 2005
by Beverly A. Potter, Ph.D.

Published by

RONIN Publishing, Inc.
PO Box 22900
Oakland, CA 94609
www.roninpub.com

Credits:

Cover design:	Brian Groppe	briangroppe.com
Interior desige	Bevely A. Potter	docpotter.com
Cartoons	Phil Frank	baba@sfchronicle.com
Text font:	Venus by Chank	www.chank.com

Publishing History:

Previously published as
Beating Job Burnout: How to Transform Work Pressure into Productivity
Harbor/Putnam 1980
Ace Business Library - mass market 1982
Ronin Publishing 1985
Ronin Publishing, 2nd edition 1993
Ronin Publishing, 2nd edition retitled 1998 after title was taken by NTC
    for a Paul Stevens translation.

Distributed to the trade by **Publishers Group West**
Printed in the United States of America by **United Graphics**
Library of Congress Card Number — 2005903041
Printing Number 1

Acknowledgements

Thanks to the many friends and colleagues whose encouragement helped propel the creation of this book. I especially appreciate my clients and those who attended my workshops. Many of their burnout experiences and techniques for renewing enthusiasm (with names changed, of course) are incorporated in the pages that follow. A special thanks to San Francisco Chronicle *cartoonist, Phil Frank for his fabulous creations, many of which are originals that he drew for* Overcoming Job Burnout.

Thank you also, dear reader, for putting your time and energy into this book. May it help empower you and bring you to a renewed sense of fulfillment in your work and your life.

-docpotter

Other Books by Docpotter

Table of Contents

Chapter One

The Burnout Syndrome

Without work, all life goes rotten,

But when work is soulless, life stifles and dies.

—Albert Camus

A "soulless" work day can leave you feeling drained and used up. Soulless work dampens enthusiasm until motivation is extinguished. Skills and expertise remain, but your will to perform—the spirit within you—dies. As burnout progresses your motivation, that mysterious force that gets you moving is damaged—in the worst cases, even destroyed.

Service providers like nurses, counselors, and police officers are hardest hit as they become cynical about their work and openly hostile to the very people they're dedicated to serving. Jobs that involve life or death decisions such as being a platoon captain or a heart surgeon have high burnout potential. Managers, team leaders, and others who work with people are also at high risk.

Other burnout-prone professions are those that require working under demanding time schedules such as newspaper journalism; those that require exacting attention such as air-traffic controllers; those that involve detailed work, such as proofreaders; those that are "politically incorrect" such as nuclear plant supervisors and IRS agents, for example.

Burnout is job depression—a malaise of the spirit.

No one is immune from job burnout.

Any person, in any profession, at any level can become a victim of job burnout.

ARE YOU BURNING OUT?

The question most people ask first is *"Am I burning out?"* Chances are if you're asking yourself that question, you are struggling with burnout to some degree. People who find their work invigorating and refueling are filled with enthusiasm. The question of burnout doesn't enter their minds. While these people may be experiencing a great deal of stress, their motivation to work is strong. In contrast, burnout saps motivation, and enthusiasm dies as working becomes meaningless drudgery.

AM I BURNING OUT?

Instructions: Review your life over the last six months, both at work and away from work. Then read each of the following items and rate how often it is true of you. When you're done add up your score.

Rating Scale: 1 = rarely, 2 = occasionally true, 3 = true half the time, 4 = frequently true, 5 = almost always true

---

____ 1. I feel tired even though I've gotten adequate sleep.

____ 2. I am dissatisfied with my work.

____ 3. I feel sad for no apparent reason.

____ 4. I am forgetful.

____ 5. I am irritable and snap at people.

____ 6. I avoid people at work and in my private life.

___ 7. I have trouble sleeping due to worrying about work.

___ 8. I get sick a lot more than I used to.

___ 9. My attitude about work is "why bother?"

___ 10. I get into conflicts.

___ 11. My job performance is not up to par.

___ 12. I use alcohol and/or drugs to feel better.

___ 13. Communicating with people is a strain.

___ 14. I can't concentrate on my work like I once could.

___ 15. I am bored with my work.

___ 16. I work hard but accomplish little.

___ 17. I feel frustrated with my work.

___ 18. I don't like going to work.

___ 19. Social activities are draining.

___ 20. Sex is not worth the effort.

___ 21. I watch TV most of the time when not working.

___ 22. I don't have much to look forward to in my work.

___ 23. I worry about work during off hours.

___ 24. My feelings about work interfere with my personal life.

___ 25. My work seems pointless.

Scoring:	
25 - 50	You're doing well.
51 - 75	You're okay if you take preventative action.
76 - 100	You're at risk for burnout.
101 - 125	You're burning out.

Many of the items in the quiz indicate depression. and Depression is a symptom, an emotional reaction, to certain circumstances including certain working conditions. But depression can also have an organic basis including problems of nutrition and brain chemistry. If you got a high score on the quiz, you are probably experiencing depression. If this depression is serious and unrelenting, consult your physician who can determine if there is a physical basis. Improved nutrition can have a tremendous impact upon your feelings of well-being. In some cases, your doctor may prescribe an antidepressive drug.

JOB DEPRESSION

Burnout can be likened to job depression. You may wonder how to determine if the problem is one of general depression that infects your work, or if it is job depression that infects your life. Answering this chicken-and-egg type of question is academic. If you scored high, you must take action to break out of the burnout cycle. Whether the source of your burnout is in your job or your personal life, in either case burnout is a trap because the process wears you down until it becomes too painful to act. By reading this book you're taking an important step toward overcoming burnout.

Burnout is not all-or-nothing.

There is no constant state. Like fire, motivation gets stronger and burns hotter, or diminishes and burns out. On any particular day your enthusiasm for work increases or decreases but it does not remain the same. Even the hottest fires will burn out, so we tend them—fanning, stoking, and occasionally adding another log. Like fires, we are not static. When motivation wanes, we burn out. There is no need for alarm as long as you still have fuel, know how to ignite motivation, and haven't waited too long.

SYMPTOMS

The symptoms of burnout are neither unusual nor mysterious. In fact, it's difficult to find someone consistently free of symptoms.

Consider John, an employment counselor:

I don't know what's gotten into me. I believe in what I'm doing. I want to help people. But something has happened. Like today, a woman came in for a job referral. Well, she started going over her plight, telling me all the reasons why she couldn't go to the interview. I've just heard it over and over. All the complaints and reasons why she can't get herself together and get a job. All of a sudden I was angry and I said, "Look, I've got problems, too. And they're worse than yours. I've heard your excuses over and over, and I'm sick of it!" I just don't know what's gotten into me. I guess I'm just burned out!

John's story is a common one. Those who work closely with others often seem to lose concern for the very people they are trying to assist and treat them in dehumanizing ways instead, becoming cynical, negative, and sometimes overtly hostile was this employment counselor. But burnout is by no means restricted to people who deal with other people's emotional, physical, or social problems. The kind of emotional exhaustion John described is experienced by people working in a wide variety of settings.

Loss of interest in work and emotional callousness eventually translate into organizational problems like absenteeism, substandard work, and high turnover. But more importantly, the victim of burnout can be permanently debilitated by the experience and, in extreme forms, can literally become unable to work. While work skills remain intact, burnout leaves its victim unable to become involved in the work as motivation to work is extinguished.

Burnout doesn't occur overnight.

It is a cumulative process, beginning with small warning signals that, when unheeded, can progress into a profound and lasting dread of going to work.

NEGATIVE EMOTIONS

Occasional feelings of frustration, anger, depression, dissatisfaction, and anxiety are normal. But people caught in the burnout cycle experience these negative emotions increasingly often until they become chronic. In the worst cases, people complain of a kind of emotional fatigue or depletion. While no two people respond in exactly the

same way, people tend to experience frustration first, which evolves over time into anger. In later stages we see anxiety and fear, then depression and despair.

Frustration

Life is fraught with frustration and barriers preventing us from getting what we want. In small doses frustration can be a helpful emotion, spurring us on to try new methods or to find alternative approaches so that we expand and grow. But when frustrations are continual and unsolvable, the stage is set for feelings of futility: "Why bother? There's no point. It's hopeless. I can't do anything anyway." If you often feel frustrated in carrying out the responsibilities of your job, you are experiencing an early symptom of burnout.

Consider Don, a software salesman:

I go out and get orders, which is not easy. The sales manager tells me to push quality service. So I do; but as likely as not the home office screws up in delivering the order. The company just doesn't come through with the type of service they promise. I'm caught with having to cool out another angry customer. Usually I'm successful in doing that, and he's happy in spite of the inconvenience. But I lose a lot of credibility. Sometimes customers are so annoyed

*they cancel the order and all my efforts have been for
nothing. This happens all the time and it's getting pretty
difficult for me to go out there and do my thing. It's getting
so that I don't like this company, and I don't like this job.
It's just too frustrating.*

When frustrations stem largely from the job situation,
intense feelings of dissatisfaction with the job itself can
result. Yet, many burnout victims blame themselves as they
attribute their frustrations to their own failings.

Consider Sara, a defense attorney:

*I'm here to help these people. And they have heavy prob-
lems. I'm supposed to defend them and to get them a
lighter sentence. Oh, they all want a suspended sentence, of
course! Sometimes I just don't devote myself to working
out a good defense like I should. I have a lot of tough cases
and they demand time. When one of my clients gets a bad
deal in the courtroom it nags at me, and I feel like I haven't
given it my best shot.*

Such nagging feelings of guilt exacerbate the original
frustrations. Not only is Sara feeling thwarted in her work
but she also feels she is the cause of the problem. In
extreme cases, feelings of guilt can escalate into bitter
self-revolution.

Depression

A tendency to blame yourself for problems arising out of
the job erodes your self-esteem, setting the stage for
depression.

Sara continues:

*When Willy got ten years I felt I really had to question my
ability to make a decent case. Since then I've just felt so
down all the time. I don't feel good about my work. I don't
like my clients and I hate myself for feeling that way. I
can't seem to look forward to anything any more. Things
that used to interest me, like tennis, don't any more. I don't*

*feel like doing anything. It's a major effort to get up and
make it through the day. I spend most weekends watching
the tube and dreading Monday morning.*

Coping with constant feelings of negativity and futility
can run down the emotional batteries of even the most
enthusiastic person. The result is feelings of profound
depression and a kind of emotional and spiritual exhaustion
where you feel like you're running on one watt, unable to
recharge. While depression may begin as a response to a
job situation, it can become a problem in itself, leading to
poor health and impaired work performance.

INTERPERSONAL PROBLEMS

The negative emotions characteristic of burnout usually
affect relationships. Feeling emotionally drained makes
interacting with people more difficult, both on the job and
at home. When inevitable conflicts arise, burnout victims
tend to overreact with emotional out-
bursts or intense hostility, making
communication with coworkers,
friends, and family increasingly
difficult.

Sara, the defense attorney, continues:

*I just don't know what's the matter
with me. All in all I like my staff.
They're a good group, and they work
hard. I don't want to but I get
cranky. It's my intention to say
something nice, yet I'm critical.
Or a couple of them will come in
laughing and joking after lunch,
and I snap or shoot a dirty look.
I don't want to be like this because it
doesn't show the way I really feel about
them. Irritation just pops out. Then I hate
myself and wonder what I'm doing in this
job.*

Moodiness and irritability over trivial provocations signal impending burnout. You experience a feeling of emotional tautness, as if the slightest inconvenience is enough to make you snap. The process is similar to overloading an electrical circuit: One additional demand for energy, no matter how small, blows a fuse. Emotional overloading makes interacting with others precarious. Getting along with people requires tolerance and patience, but tolerance level drops as the burnout grows.

Interpersonal disturbances are not restricted to working relationships, however. In fact, difficulties may appear in your private life first. Frustrating, conflicting relationships put additional strain on emotional circuits, creating even more frequent blowouts. We need emotional support. An unsatisfactory personal encounter combined with job frustration can set you up for an emotional meltdown.

Emotional Withdrawal

People suffering from job burnout tend to withdraw from social interactions. This tendency is most pronounced among helping professionals who often become aloof and inaccessible to the very people they are expected to help.

John, an employment counselor, says:

I just feel emotionally empty. I listen to people's problems I can't solve all day long. I do the best I can to offer support and empathy but lately it's getting harder to do. I listen to awful things and feel nothing — like today when Alicia told me what her uncle did to her when she was six. I felt nothing, not even outrage.

When I'm not with clients I close my door so none of the other staff will come in to talk. I know I should be interested in people around here but listening to them complain about their case loads and problems with their kids takes too much energy. I used to look forward to the Friday TGIF get-togethers. Now I just go home.

People tend to defend themselves against adverse job situations by emotionally withdrawing. But this short-term solution only accelerates burnout because a strong social support system acts like a buffer against burnout. Nonetheless, people caught in the burnout cycle withdraw. By cutting themselves off from friends and colleagues they deprive themselves of the support they desperately need.

Emotional withdrawal is common among people in the service professions, like John, the employment counselor. Others such as managers and team leaders who work closely with people often suffer similar symptoms. A natural response is indifference to the people's feelings and problems.

Dehumanization is common. Many helpers begin to think of their clients not as people but as objects. Others will respond to the drain on their emotions with hostility as John did. Still others become aloof and intellectual, talking about their clients as abstract cases in a textbook. All of these attempts to cope actually accelerate the burnout process. When going to work becomes increasingly unpleasant, it becomes an endurance test. A nearly complete emotional shutdown will eventually occur.

HEALTH PROBLEMS

As burnout victims' emotional reserves are depleted and the quality of relationships deteriorates, their physical resilience declines. They are in state of chronic tension or stress. Minor ailments, such as colds, headaches, insomnia and backaches become more frequent. There is a general feeling of being tired and rundown.

Don, the software salesman, continues:

I've always thought of myself as a healthy person, but when I look at my track record over this year, I really can't claim that any more. These days it seems like if there's a bug going around I'm sure to get it. This winter I've already had three colds. Hell, I've had the same cold all winter long! And I've been getting indigestion. But that's probably from the tension on the job. What bothers me most is my trouble sleeping. Maybe one night a week I get fairly decent sleep but the rest of the time I toss and turn all night. I just can't get the job out of my head.

Frustration, feelings of guilt, interpersonal conflicts, and even depression are all stressors. In addition to these, burnout victims must also contend with continual physical tension. Burnout takes a physical toll. Burnout victims have more than their share of health problems, from colds, flus, and allergy attacks, to insomnia, cardiovascular and gastrointestinal breakdowns, and other serious health problems.

SELF-MEDICATION

As the occupational "blahs" become chronic, many burnouts seek chemical solutions to overwhelming emotional demands and stresses. People often drink more alcohol, eat more or eat less and use drugs such as sleeping pills, tranquilizers, and mood elevators. Chain smoking and drinking large amounts of coffee and sugar are also common. This increased substance abuse further compounds health problems.

Sara, the defense attorney, continues:

My using drugs started out because I was so demoralized about work. Just despondent, really. What happened was I couldn't sleep. I'd be miserable and I'd think about things that happened at work. I'd lie awake for hours, and then I'd be exhausted in the morning. I talked to my doctor about it and he gave me some kind of pill to perk me up. And that worked, I guess. Only, well, then I still couldn't sleep because of the pill. So he gave me a pill to put me to sleep. Now, I'm totally caught in this thing. I take something to go to sleep, and I take something to wake up.

People suffering burnout often use substances in an attempt to self-medicate their anxiety and depression. Not only doesn't this help to alleviate the underlying causes of these distressing feelings, but addiction becomes a risk. If the person does develop a chemical dependency, then the symptoms of addiction add another layer to the person's problems, making it even more difficult to overcome.

DECLINING PERFORMANCE

High energy level, good health, and enthusiasm—the necessary conditions for peak performance—are all depleted in burnout. A person may become bored and unable to get excited about projects, or in other cases, the burnout victims may discover that concentrating on projects is increasingly difficult. In both cases efficiency suffers and quality of output declines.

As work becomes more painful and less rewarding, absenteeism is likely to increase. Even when physically present, the burnout victim is often emotionally and mentally absent from the job. Health problems, substance abuse and interpersonal strain makes it difficult to extend oneself to coworkers and others at work whose cooperation and goodwill are needed to get the job done. As others pull back from the burnout victim, it becomes harder for the person to perform optimally because a solid social support system is generally required for high performance. So it is only a matter of time until there is a substantial drop in the quality of performance. The result is a decline in productivity.

Don, the software engineer, continues:

I used to be one of those red-hot go-getters. I could sell anything to anyone. I was passionate about my work. I took it home with me. I slept with it. I thought about it all the time. I loved it. Now, I've run down. The job has so many frustrations and demands. I don't feel like the same person any more. I go into the office and I don't even care if I do a good job. I just put in my time. I know that the quality of my work has dropped. If I think about it, I feel like hell, so I just don't think about it! I ought to get out of here. But I don't have enough energy to look for another job. I figure I'm really not doing anything here anyway. They're paying me to do nothing, so I tell myself, "I think I'll just stay home today."

FEELINGS OF MEANINGLESSNESS

If you're like most people, you want more from your job than a pay check. You probably want to feel that you are doing something meaningful—that what you did on the job serves an important purpose. Unfortunately for burnout victims, working can become meaningless, as they question if working accomplishes anything important.

A strong signal that the burnout victim is sliding into an existential crisis of meaninglessness is evident when statements about work are cloaked with a "So what?" or "Why bother?" attitude.

**So What?
Why bother?**

This is particularly striking among burnout victims who were once very enthusiastic and dedicated. Enthusiasm is replaced by cynicism. Working seems pointless.

VICIOUS CYCLE

The burnout syndrome takes on a life of its own. Feelings of futility, disappointment, and guilt provoke interpersonal hassles and depression. Emotionally drained, health problems can set in and performance ultimately drops. As performance deteriorates, there is an even greater sense of futility and guilt. A vicious cycle becomes entrenched. Eventually painful emotions give way to lethargy. The person cannot muster enough energy to participate in life; talents remain dormant, knowledge untapped, and potential squandered. The vital driving force has become a whimper. As a malaise of the spirit, burnout attacks and depletes motivation. The cycle rarely stops by itself.

In desperation, the burnout victim may quit one job to seek another. But beginning a new job without first understanding the problem with the first job is a setup for another disaster. It is easy to unwittingly get into another job with the same problems. Essentially, the new job picks up where the first one left off. Then the second job may promote burnout even more rapidly in the face of fewer frustrations. The burnout victim may once again seek another job, only to find a repeat performance and eventually become unable to work at all.

Chapter Two

Causes of Burnout

Burnout has both physical and psychological effects but it is neither a physical ailment nor a neurosis. Burnout is a motivational problem. It attacks the will; enthusiasm wanes, motivation is damaged, resulting in an inability to mobilize interest and capabilities.

Just as the body needs vitamins and protein for optimal health, certain "nutrients" are also essential to sustain high motivation: Positive consequences or "wins" for good work and feeling you can control things that influence you nourish motivation and help prevent burnout.

WINS FOR GOOD WORK

If your motivation is to remain high, you must get positive consequences or "wins" for performing. Suppose, for example, you take work home from the office and upon discovering this your boss unexpectedly gives you Friday afternoon off. You'll probably experience this as a win for having worked at home, and your motivation to take work home will probably stay strong. If, on the other hand, your boss criticizes you, saying you're an incompetent who can't get the job done during work hours, chances are you'll stop working at home.

Positive Wins

Wins can be positive or negative. A "positive win" occurs when you do something and something positive occurs as a result. For example, suppose you make a sale and then you get a bonus. The bonus is a win. If you complete an assignment on time and feel satisfied, your good feeling is a win. If a colleague tells you that you look good in a new outfit, the compliment is a win. Wins such as these fuel motivation to repeat the winning actions.

Negative Wins

Not all wins are positive, however. An action that turns off something negative is a win. For example, suppose you have a headache, which feels bad, so you take an aspirin and the headache stops. You just experienced a negative win. Another example of a negative win is when an employee is socializing instead of working (negative situation) so you chew him out and the employee stops (negative disappears). In both examples, you experienced a win when a negative was removed. Such wins promote motivation in a negative away.

It feels so good when I stop.

A negative win is like the old joke where a man, who is banging his head against a wall, says, "Oh, this really hurts!" A second man asks, "Why are you doing that?" and the first man replies, "Because it feels so good when I stop!"

Punishment

When you perform but receive no wins, motivation will usually suffer, especially when you expected a win. Suppose you spend several hours cleaning up the office and putting away stacks of paper. You expect your business partner to be pleased but instead she says nothing about the tidy office and doesn't even seem to notice at all. Chances are you will be less likely to straighten up the office in the future.

When you perform and are punished, motivation will almost always decline. For example, suppose after working all weekend on a proposal, your boss frowns, flips through it, points to a word and says, "You misspelled this word." You'll probably experience this response as punitive and motivation to work on weekends will evaporate.

WINS AND MOTIVATION

While positive and negative wins keep motivation high, they are not equal. Positive wins generate "working for" motivation, whereas negative wins generate "working to avoid" motivation.

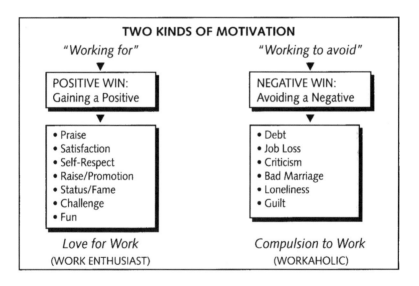

Positive wins promote motivation to work for positives, which generate work enthusiasm or a love for work. Positive wins include praise, feelings of satisfaction, high self-esteem, raises, bonuses, promotions, fame, credibility, challenge, adventure, fun, and anything else that is positive to you. Negative wins promote motivation to work to avoid negatives, which leads to workaholism or a compulsion to work. Negative wins include avoiding criticism, alleviating loneliness, reducing debts, turning off fear, avoiding guilt, getting away from bad relationships, and avoiding anything else that you find punitive and unpleasant.

In both cases the person is motivated but for different reasons. Workaholism is propelled by fear-based decisions—decisions aimed at *avoiding* unpleasant situations; whereas work enthusiasts work for enjoyment. Working for pulls work enthusiasts towards desirable wins; while working to avoid pushes workaholics away from negatives and through the toil and drudgery.

TIMING OF WINS

Timing of a win has an impact upon its power to sustain motivate. The sooner the win, the more powerful. A win, such as recognition, that comes weeks or months after performance of a laudable deed has less impact than if it were received immediately.

Consider Steve, a scientist:

I worked for months on an electronic switching system. It was interesting at first. But it became paper—just so much paper. Now three years later they tell me they're going to use the system. I suppose I should feel good. But I can't get much satisfaction from it. That project was so far in the past what good is recognition now? It doesn't really mean anything to me.

When there is a long delay between work and wins, you can feel unrewarded even when the wins finally do come. Such "devices" as the Christmas bonus are meant to be an acknowledgment for good work, for example. Unfortunately, if the good work occurred in the middle of the summer and the recognition doesn't come until Christmas, the bonus does little to fuel motivation. Sometimes it can even backfire, such as when employees expect the bonus and then are angry when they don't get one or when it is less than hoped for.

FEELINGS OF CONTROL

When we feel in control, we relax because we have an understanding how to get wins we want and avoid negatives we don't want. When we are unsuccessful in discovering causal relationship between our behavior (if I do this) and the world's response (then I can expect that) we can feel helpless to influence what happens to us.

Consider Ann, a broadcast executive:

When I go on a tour of stations in my region, Burt, my training supervisor, goes with me. I can't do anything right. He doesn't like the way I park the car, the way I put the luggage in the trunk, the way I hand the money to the toll collector on the bridge. It's just one constant criticism. I know these are trivial matters, but it wears me down and I get so tense. He brushes aside what I do well with no comment.

Recently I spent a whole weekend putting together a presentation for a station manager. I wanted to show him I can do a good job. I know this business and I do good work. Burt wanted to see the outline of what I was going to present. After he looked at it he said nothing. The presentation was well received. The whole staff was excited and the station manager signed a new contract.

In my evaluation Burt said I needed to improve my "speaking skills" and omitted that I had sold a new contract. He made me sound like a failure. I feel like giving up. What's the point in trying? No matter what I do, it's wrong. So why knock myself out?

Ann desires to be acknowledged by receiving compliments or some other type of positive feedback for her efforts but she has been unsuccessful in figuring out what she must do to get a positive response from her boss.

Feeling helpless—sense of uncontrollability—engenders a sense of futility. We must believe we are potent, that we have the power to influence what happens to us. I say "believe" because how we see the world exerts a significant impact upon our susceptibility to burnout. Any time you perceive the important aspects of your worklife as uncontrollable, you are in trouble.

A sense of futility develops.

Research suggests, for example, that Voodoo deaths may be caused because the victims believed they were helpless. Many concentration-camp prisoners seemed to have died of helplessness. They were told and believed that the environment—the guards—had total power over them. Based on his own experience, Bruno Bettleheim, a renowned psychologist who survived one of the worst Nazi death camps, says that it was when people gave up trying to influence what happened to them that they became "walking corpses."

LEARNED HELPLESSNESS

Psychologist Martin Seligman spent years studying the impact of "controllability" on people and animals. In a typical study matched pairs of dogs were divided into two groups. In the "controllable" situation, a naive dog was placed in a room with an electric grid floor that contained a puzzle. If the dog "solved" the puzzle, such as pushing a lever, the shock stopped.

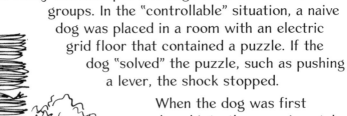

When the dog was first placed into the experimental room it was relaxed and friendly as it wagged its tail and wiggled its nose. However, when the electric floor was activated, the dog's demeanor changed dramatically. It jumped and yelped as it ran around as it frantically searching for a way out. Eventually the dog accidentally pushed the lever, causing the shock to stop — a powerful negative win. Over the next several trials when the dog was put back in the room and the shock turned on, the dog quickly learned to push the lever. The dog was highly motivated—albeit by "working to avoid" pain. The dog learned that it could do something to control its world.

In the "uncontrollable" situation, a second dog was placed in the same room with the electric floor, only this time there was no puzzle, which when solved turned off the shock. Just like the first dog, when shocked it ran around trying to find a way out. When the dog understood that there was nothing it could do it dog gave up, stopped trying and took the shock. The second dog learned that it was helpless.

Impaired Ability to Learn

Next, the second dog that had learned that it was helpless was put into the room with the lever (the controllable situation) but it made no effort to find a way out. Instead the dog just lay on the floor and took the shock. Even when the door was left wide open, the dog did not attempt to escape the shock. The dog could not seem to learn that the conditions had changed and that it was no longer helpless. The second dog "learned" that it was helpless and stopped trying to get away.

Negative Emotions

The helpless dog exhibited negative emotions: first yelping and growling, later whimpering, and eventually just remaining motionless. Powerlessness at work can affect people in the same way. As they learn that there is nothing they can do they experience negative emotions, beginning with frustration and anger, later anxiety and guilt, and eventually depression and despair. In the process, motivation declines. When the conditions change they can't seem to learn and so they continue acting helpless.

Diminished Motivation

When the second dog "learned" that it was helpless its motivation to help itself was impaired. It just lay there and took the shock. Of course, scientists can't subject people to such experiments so we have no direct scientific data on the effects of powerlessness on human subjects. However, we can speculate that the battered-wife syndrome may be caused by learned helplessness, for example. If the woman believes that she is powerless before an abusive husband, she will probably act like the dog on the grid floor, taking the abuse and not running away when she has the opportunity.

People in ghettos who don't avail themselves of opportunities, such as educational programs, may fail to do so not because of laziness, but because they have learned that they are helpless and, as a result, cannot act. Homeless people who are skilled and were once securely employed but now are unable to hold a job, may also be victims of learned helplessness. People who are chronically depressed may have become so as a result of feelings of powerlessness.

In his research, Seligman discovered that animals who learn to be helpless have little resistance to adverse situations. They often die in as few as ten minutes when placed in a survival situation, whereas animals who have learned mastery continue fighting to survive hours later. This and other research suggests learned helplessness is literally life-threatening and even triggers a biological suicide mechanism. In some cases biological functions simply slow down or cease; other studies indicate that the body may develop a terminal disease. This is supported by research with cancer patients that suggested that people who are depressed and feel like victims were more likely to get cancer.

LOW RESISTANCE TO ADVERSITY.

An uncontrollable situation can be harmful without being physically painful. Feeling helpless can do serious damage to motivation in any situation, even those filled with luxury and privilege.

Consider Bob:

I'm a VIP. That's my title. I have a plush office and I make a lot of money! It's my father's company, and the way Dad treats me has been the same since I was a child. He streamrolls in and handles everything for me. Once when I was eight I remember deliberately breaking a window. Dad paid for it right away. I didn't so much as get a whack on the ass. I've had everything I wanted—whether I wanted it or not! Dad got me into the top business school in spite of my "weak" academic record. You know, the Good Old Boys' Club? Well, he's president.

I resisted working here, but Dad let me know that if I wanted to continue enjoying the pleasures I'm accustomed to I'd better reconsider. Hell, why bother fighting the old goat? So here I am. When I first started, I tried to put into action some of my ideas and make some changes and start some programs. But Dad, as always, came right in and "fixed" things. Why bother? If he wants to pay me for nothing, it's his money. I go on a lot of business trips, and I meet a lot of foxy women. It's not a bad life at all. I don't get ulcers. Let Dad worry about the market, production, and the board. I enjoy myself!

Surprisingly, Bob's situation is similar to Ann's. While Ann is overloaded with criticism and Bob has an overabundance of occupational goodies, both lack a sense of control. Neither feel they can influence what happens to them. Seligman emphasizes in his research on learned helplessness that it is not the quality of the situation that causes feelings of helplessness and depression. Even though we tend to think that the cause is punitive

circumstances, situations filled with rewards can also lead to the same debilitating learned helplessness and depression when the person does not have to perform to get those rewards. Seligman describes research with rats and pigeons in which they could choose between getting food free and having to make certain responses to get the same food. The rats and pigeons choose to work!

As feelings of powerlessness continue, Ann and Bob will both become candidates for depression. Both will probably experience a dramatic drop in motivation to continue trying to command their respective worlds. Having learned that their efforts cannot influence the world, Ann and Bob may opt for simply plodding along. As the quality of their performance drops, it will feed depression and the vicious cycle will have begun.

VICIOUS CYCLE

Burnout erodes in insidious ways. Most detrimental is the way that experiencing uncontrollability tends to undermine motivation to learn in new situations. Ann and Bob have learned that they can't control their respective worlds so they stop trying to do so, which handicaps their ability to adapt—to learn. In this way burnout victims become psychologically "crippled" and burnout becomes chronic.

When Bob and Ann stop looking for ways to control their respective oppressors, they will stop finding them. Their own self-imposed "blindness" will keep them helpless. They will remain helpless because they feel helpless. If, for example, Ann's boss underwent an intensive manage-

ment-training program and developed good supervisory skills, Ann may, nonetheless, continue to expect her efforts to be futile. Because of her negative expectations of him, she would probably not be inclined to try her hardest and would therefore provide Burt with little to acknowledge. Even if she were to be presented with evidence that he had changed, she might not see the changes. That is, if Burt acknowledged her performance, she might still discount it as an exception: "Oh, he was just in a good mood. He'll think of something to get me on later."

The same might be true for Bob. If his father retired, Bob's years of training in helplessness will still remain with him, probably causing Bob to continue to tell himself it is futile to attempt to grab the reins. Having learned not to expect a relationship between his actions and their outcomes, he would probably continue to interpret the world as uncontrollable.

Defeated people see only defeat, never success, and thereby remain defeated.

Once a defeatist attitude is learned, it clings tenaciously. Yet, there are ways to escape from the negative trap of job burnout. The root cause of burnout is the feeling of helplessness and the perception that there is nothing you can do. Burnout is prevented by an "I-Can-Do" attitude—a feeling of potency, the belief that there is something "I can do." But before we go into the paths to personal power, let's look at specific kinds of situations that can engender feelings of helplessness.

Chapter Three

Burnout Situations

*E*very job has demotivating aspects. But real "killer jobs" have a preponderance of burnout-promoting situations. The Japanese even coined the term *karoshi* for "death by over work". Similar burnout promoting situations come up again and again in working with people in all stages of burnout and recovery. The Burnout Potential Inventory surveys these burnout-promoting situations.

BURNOUT POTENTIAL INVENTORY

Instructions: Rate how often each situation bothers you at work. Use a scale from 1 to 9 to rate the situations, one at a time, with 1 being "rarely," and 9 being "constantly." Add up the ratings to get your score.

POWERLESSNESS

____ 1. I can't solve the problems assigned to me.

____ 2. I am trapped in my job with no options.

____ 3. I am unable to influence decisions that affect me.

____ 4. I may be laid off and there is nothing I can do about it.

INADEQUATE INFORMATION

____ 5. I am unclear on the scope and responsibilities of my job.

____ 6. I don't have information I need to perform well.

____ 7. People I work with don't understand my role.

____ 8. I don't understand the purpose of my work.

CONFLICT

____ 9. I am caught in the middle.

____ 10. I must satisfy conflicting demands.

____ 11. I disagree with people at work.

____ 12. I must violate procedures in order to get my job done.

POOR TEAM WORK

____ 13. Coworkers undermine me.

____ 14. Management displays favoritism.

____ 15. Office politics interfere with my doing my job.

____ 16. People compete instead of cooperate.

OVERLOAD

____ 17. My job interferes with my personal life.

____ 18. I have too much to do and too little time to do it.

____ 19. I must work on my own time.

____ 20. The amount of work interferes with how well I do it.

BOREDOM

____ 21. I have too little to do.

____ 22. I am overqualified for the work I actually do.

____ 23. My work is not challenging.

____ 24. The majority of my time is spent on routine tasks.

POOR FEEDBACK

____ 25. I don't know what I am doing right or wrong.

____ 26. I don't know what my supervisor thinks of my work.

____ 27. I get information too late to act on it.

____ 28. I don't see the results of my work.

PUNISHMENT

____ 29. My supervisor is critical.

____ 30. Someone else gets credit for my work.

____ 31. My work is unappreciated.

____ 32. I get blamed for others' mistakes.

ALIENATION

___ 33. I am isolated from others.

___ 34. I'm just a cog in the organizational wheel.

___ 35. I don't have much in common with my coworkers.

___ 36. I avoid telling people where I work or what I do.

AMBIGUITY

___ 37. The rules are constantly changing.

___ 38. I don't know what is expected of me.

___ 39. There's no relationship between performance and success.

___ 40. Priorities I must meet are unclear.

UNREWARDING

___ 41. My work is not satisfying.

___ 42. I have few real successes.

___ 43. My career progress is not what I'd hoped.

___ 44. I don't get respect.

VALUE CONFLICT

___ 45. I must compromise my values.

___ 46. People disapprove of what I do.

___ 47. I don't believe in the company.

___ 48. My heart is not in my work.

Scoring:	Your Risk of Burnout
48 - 168	Low: Take preventative action.
169 - 312	Moderate: Develop a plan to correct problem areas.
313 - 432	High: Corrective action is vital.

There are many situations that can cause even the most motivated person to experience burnout. In each case, the ingredients required to sustain high motivation are lacking.

CRITICAL BOSS

The broadcast executive whose boss ignored her proposal
and pooh-poohed her presentation is a good example of
the critical boss. Some criticism is helpful because it lets
us know what to improve. But in Ann's situation her boss,
Burt, was miserly in giving her even the smallest acknowledgment despite her efforts and good performance. She
felt helpless because no matter what she did or how she
did it Burt always found something to find fault with. When
she asked him directly what she might do to improve her
performance, Burt criticized her for asking.

Ann, the broadcast executive, continues

*The News Service automatically renews its contracts unless
the contractor puts in a notice of cancellation. You can see
the problem. It's easy to forget about it and then discover
that the service has been automatically renewed. Some
station managers protect themselves by putting in a notice
of cancellation immediately after signing the contract. This
is logical and, having been a general manager myself, I
understand it. This is exactly what one of my clients did.
"Ann," he said, "I'm satisfied with the service, but I've
placed a cancellation notice to protect myself. It's routine. I
always do this, so don't take it personally. I'll probably
renew." Naturally, I gave him the standard arguments
against his decision, but he was insistent. Afterward, Burt
berated me for having accepted the notice. I told him I gave
my client all the arguments in the training manual as well
as some I'd picked up from the seasoned people.
He wouldn't listen, and contin-
ued with his harangue. Finally,
in desperation I asked him
what I should have done.
You know what he said?
"Ann, if you don't
know now, you
never will!" Now I
ask you, what kind
of answer is that?
I'm ready to give up.
There's nothing I can
do right.*

Perhaps Burt thinks Ann is a threat to his job; or perhaps he finds having a woman as a broadcast executive unsettling; or there may be something about Ann's personality that he finds particularly grating; or perhaps Burt thinks negativity is a good motivator. Whatever the reason for Burt's one-sidedness, the basic lesson for Ann is that there can be no way she can succeed. While the failing may actually be Burt's, it is Ann and the news service that suffer. As Ann loses her motivation, her performance and well-being can be expected to take an abrupt nose-dive. The news service loses a good performer.

Sometimes the constant criticism is not from a boss but from a customer or partner. The result is the same: You come to feel that there is no way you can satisfy the person. No matter what you do, he or she finds fault. You can't win and wonder, why bother even trying?

PERFECTIONISM

To perfectionists, only perfection is acceptable and anything less is inadequate. Working with a perfectionist—who could be your boss, a coworker, or partner—is difficult for most people because no one can meet the perfectionist's standards. Perfectionists focus on rooting out imperfection, no matter how small. They ignore progress and what has been done well to instead attack what they see as imperfect. Since no one can be perfect—especially on a continual basis—perfectionists deal out constant criticism, which is demotivating. A subordinate or partner has the choice, at least in principle, of leaving the perfectionist. But when you are the perfectionist you are stuck with the worst kind of critical boss—inside your head!

LACK OF RECOGNITION

A simple lack of recognition can erode enthusiasm for working. Suppose you spend a lot of time and energy preparing a report which, when completed, sits for days on your supervisor's desk untouched. How will this affect your motivation?

Consider Gregory, a civil servant:

I guess I need those pats on the back. I wish I could be a mover. I used to work hard. And, you know, I enjoyed it. That's when I was in school. I guess it was grades I worked for. Now, I've lost my spirit. I come to work and I do my work and I go home. Nothing comes back. There's no reflection in the mirror. I sometimes wonder if I exist. It's silly to expect anything. It's the government and I'm not special. God knows that! But I can't keep it up—working in a vacuum like this. So I just don't try as hard as I used to. And I still get paid. That's the funny thing. I suppose I should just accept it. Sometimes I think of getting another job. But civil service gives security. And to tell it straight, I just don't have what it takes to get out there and be aggressive. Maybe I never did. I don't like my job very much, though, and it's getting pretty hard for me to keep it up. I miss that old enthusiasm but I just don't have what it takes any more.

Desperation and powerlessness are evident in Gregory's words. He feels it is futile to seek what he needs. He even blames and berates himself for needing recognition. Gregory is another burned-out bureaucrat, perfunctorily carrying out his job. His usefulness to the organization is greatly diminished. What's worse, he is damaged by the experience. He feels stuck in it, unable to perform and unable to leave to find a more satisfying work environment.

Many managers assume that the paycheck is all people need to sustain peak performance. Many supervisors are stingy with their recognition as if these were rare and finite commodities; others righteously boast that they recognize only outstanding performance. Unfortunately, good performance and improving performance goes unacknowledged, reducing motivation to reach outstanding performance.

Inadequate Pay

When you work hard but feel underpaid, you can feel your efforts and outputs are not being adequately recognized. People spend years in college believing it will lead to personal recognition and well-paid work. If they are paid less than what they had expected, it can be viewed as lack of respect because pay is often used as an indicator of "respect." This can feel punitive and lead to alienation, especially when there is a poor match between the work and the person's values.

Traditionally women have been paid less than men doing the same work. Many women hope to get equal pay through professional training and advanced degrees only to find that they are still paid only about 70 percent of their male counterparts. An ambitious woman can develop a feeling of helplessness when her experience teaches her that no matter how hard she works or how well she performs she'll receive significantly less pay and recognition than a man in the next office who may not work as hard or perform as well.

Under-Employment

If you have high aspirations and spent years in college preparing for work but are employed below your appropriate level, you can equate this with a lack of recognition. Women are often underemployed. It is not uncommon, for example, to find a woman lawyer doing the work of a law clerk or paralegal. Stories abound of Ph.D.s who work in the Post Office because they can't find a college teaching job. Recent graduates with liberal arts majors often discover they have few marketable skills and must work as waiters and waitresses. People who have been laid off when their companies were downsizing and have had to take jobs below their capabilities can similarly suffer from lack of recognition and be prone to burnout. Many who soared during the dot.com era find themselves going from one under-skilled "gig" to another as they scrap by on a fraction of their former salary.

AMBIGUITY

Ambiguity can diminish self-confidence. If you don't know what's expected, it is difficult to feel confident that you are doing the right thing in the right way. Ambiguity is fraught with potential for criticism, especially with a supervisor like Burt.

Consider Rick, a top executive:

Getting this job was a terrific opportunity, and I was thrilled to have it. But I've had a problem getting a handle on the job and it's been a frustrating experience. Samuels— he's the president—built the place up from a one-man operation. Well, he never fills me in on the big picture. I get a piece of it but never enough. Like the grant proposal last month. I worked on that for weeks, and I thought every- thing was coming together. I was feeling real good—finally. Betty was doing a terrific job on the research, and Allen conducted a couple dozen interviews. Then Samuels tells me that the grant isn't a priority project at all. He wants us to put it on the back burner and to move on the Andar project. I felt really deflated. I worked and I cared—all for nothing. I didn't even get to present my proposal to him. He wouldn't even listen to a summary. This is not an isolated incident. I'm constantly in the dark. I don't know which way I'm going, and I can't pin him down. Lately I've had trouble concentrating. I can't focus. I'm really tense, and I spend a lot of time worrying about my competence.

Rick faces unclear goals and objectives. He doesn't know the parameters and scope of his job, what direction he is expected to go in, how his function fits in with the overall organizational goals, or even what the organiza- tional goals are. Rick needs information. Without sufficient information to make decisions and set priorities, he cannot perform the job adequately. His energy and motivation are dissipated in futile, endless trial and error. Ambiguity dampens motivation because insufficient information makes successful performance unlikely. Like Ann, Rick is going through a period of frustration that will probably become futility because he feels powerless.

Information is power. Samuels has a corner on the power and regardless of his intentions, is keeping Rick powerless by withholding the information he needs to perform. Whatever Samuels's motivation—powerlust or inability to delegate—the result is the same for Rick. He is rendered unable to work effectively. Ambiguity is often caused by a supervisor not knowing how to develop clear goals and objectives or how to communicate them to his workers.

TASKS WITH NO END

In Greek mythology, Susyphus was an evil king condemned to Hades to forever roll a big rock up a mountain. Each day he strained and struggled, pushing the heavy rock up the steep mountain until he finally made it to the top. Each night, as he slept, the rock rolled back down to the bottom of the mountain. Susyphus's task never ended.

In today's workplace many people's jobs fits this picture of Hell. Secretaries struggle all day to empty their in-baskets, only to find them full again the next day. People with clients who don't get better can have a similar experience. Eventually, they can develop feelings of futility: "No matter how hard I work or how late I stay at the office, I just can't make any headway in my job." Every day they push the rock up the mountain only to find it back on their desks again the next day.

Entrepreneurs, sole practitioners, and others who are self-employed easily fall prey to tasks without end. Any project or business of substance can't be accomplished in a day, a week, or even a month. Employees, however, can set aside work at the end of their shift—whether or not it has been completed. People who are their own boss tend to push themselves to complete work, regardless of how long it takes. The self-employed typically work many more hours a week than do their employees, for less pay than their employed counterparts. While employees expect paid holidays and vacations, the self-employed often go for years, even decades without a vacation. Their business becomes a task without end.

IMPOSSIBLE TASKS

Impossible tasks are similar to the problem of ambiguity in that a person is not able to perform an assigned task. Unlike ambiguity, however, where lack of information or conflicting messages makes performing difficult, with an impossible task it is clear what is supposed to be accomplished—it is just not possible to do so.

Sara, the defense attorney, continues:

I have to go to court today to defend a guy on three counts of selling heroin. It's a hopeless case because the guy sold the stuff to two separate police agents. His only defense is: "I didn't do it. I never saw those guys before." His attitude is totally unreasonable. He's not willing to make a deal. So obviously he's going to be convicted and get the maximum sentence. And I'm caught in the middle. I'm trapped between a client who won't cooperate and the people who want to pinch him. I'm his defense attorney, and there's no significant defense. Well, it's very frustrating.

Sara's job is to defend people who are being accused of having committed crimes, for which they have no real defense. In many of her cases, the client is clearly guilty and often uncooperative—don't show up for appointments and court appearances, withhold information, and at times, lie to her. To make matters worse, the size of Sara's caseload precludes her from preparing an adequate defense even when one is possible. There are simply too many defenses to be made. Moreover, the courts and other agencies present other hurdles that compound matters further. In short, it is impossible for Sara to do her job well. Variations of Sara's situation are confronted by helping professionals every day.

Incurable Clients

Many service providers, such as social workers, and public guardians, have large caseloads of clients with nearly impossible problems. No matter how hard they try, how much they give or how much they care, the drug addicts continue to use drugs, the welfare recipients can't get work, and the delinquents end up back in juvenile hall.

Consider Frank, a rehab counselor:

I work on a hospital ward with drug abusers. I used to find the work fulfilling. I threw myself into it. I cared about those guys. I worked with them, and there were results, or so I thought. A couple would start to shape up, develop some skills, and become more responsible. They'd look good. And after several months of intensive work, it would sometimes be difficult to tell them from the staff. Finally, they'd graduate from the program. I'd have high expectations and felt good. I'd helped them! They'd go out into the world and last about three months at the most. Then one day I'd be in detox and there they'd be again.

I'll never forget the first time it happened. Billy Wagner. I put my soul into that guy. And there he was looking exactly the same as he did eight months before when I saw him in detox the first time. I was shattered. He'd done so well. If anyone could make it, he could. Only he didn't. And he's typical. I don't believe people can change anymore. I think these guys are doomed to a lifetime of this and there's not one thing I or anyone else can do. I don't get involved anymore. I can't take it. I'm burning out. It rips my guts out. I know they won't make it, yet I've got to go into the ward every day and convince them that they can.

When people helpers are able to provide genuine relief-giving assistance, it can be profoundly satisfying. But when they can't do a thing, it becomes a kind of emotional assault and battery. Burnout symptoms result from attempts to cope with the emotional fatigue that results.. Emotional withdrawal is common. Turning on their clients, blaming them for their plight is common. Becoming cold and callous is another attempt to cope with the emotional drain. Others turn into rule-worshiping bureaucrats.

Consider Jackson, a case worker:

I work with the homeless and the near homeless. It's my job to rehabilitate them. I'm expected to wave some sort of magic wand and get them to pull their lives together, get off the bottle, get a job or into a training program and set up housekeeping somewhere. My caseload is over 250 people, so I don't have enough time in a day to see each of my clients even once a month.

These people are damaged goods. They'll never live normal lives. And it'd cost tens of thousands of dollars to "rehabilitate" them. My budget is ridiculous. I have about $100 per person. Maybe I'm cynical, but it's a reality. So I'm suppose to single-handedly make them right? Well, it's a joke—a sick joke! I've got to sit here every day and somehow face these people who come to me to help them. I can't help. So maybe I get them into a flophouse for a week. Maybe I get them a two-week meal ticket. Then what?

NO WIN SITUATIONS

Closely related to the impossible task is the "no-win" situation. With the impossible task you are expected to do the impossible, whereas in the no-win situation you are presented with demands that are possible to achieve but mutually exclusive. This motivation extinguisher can take a number of forms.

**If you can't win
it is natural to stop trying.**

Incompatible Demands

Incompatible demands means that satisfying one results in failing to satisfy another. Further, you are expected to satisfy both demands. Actually, it is a lose-lose situation because there is no way you can win. Every time you win, you simultaneously lose. These kinds of situations are often called damned-if-you-do damned-if-you-don't because no matter what you do you are "damned."

If you report to two bosses you can be confronted with incompatible demands. One boss may want speed while the other wants quality, for example. Producing both may not be possible. Jobs that require working across departmental boundaries are also plagued by incompatible demands. Marketing wants one thing while manufacturing wants another. Anyone interfacing between unions and management struggles with this problem.

Consider Ralph, a machinist:

I'm the best machinist in the shop and everybody knows it. Sometimes I wish I was just an average Joe because people expect the impossible from me. It's the foreman. He wants precision work. And I can do precision work. He wants me to cut to an accuracy of 1/100th of an inch, and I can do this. But quality

Now choose!

takes time. This is what I tell John, and this is what he
wants. When I take the time and I put out a top-notch
product, he turns around and gets on my back because he
wants to move items. He wants quantity. He wants speed.
He wants to get the bucks. Well, I try to explain to him that
he can have one or the other but not both. I say, "Okay,
okay, John. I'll do it. I'll work as fast as I can." I work fast
and I don't get accuracy. With speed I can maybe do cuts to
1/80th of an inch and that's damn good! But there are
complaints. The fit's not perfect. And John's down on my
case because of quality. Well, what am I suppose to do? I
tell him I'm not superman, and he doesn't understand. I
just can't win so I've stopped trying.

Ralph is in a double bind. When he satisfies John's demands for quality he fails to meet the demand for quantity; when he meets the quantity he fails to meet the demand for quality. In other words, Ralph works and works. He tries to perform as he's directed, yet he never actually receives the payoff he desires or has been promised. Basically, Ralph faces the same problem as Ann. He is continually receiving negative consequences for his performance and appears powerless to change this. A person in a losing situation will try only so long and then give up. Conflicting demands from different sources can be equally devastating.

Consider Janis, a production foreman:

I'm caught in the middle and it's hell. I get management
down on me and they want production. That's how they
make money. They want these guys working at maximum
output and if they don't it's my head on the block. So when
I go down to the production line and try to get these guys
to work harder, I run into the union steward. He's saying,
"Come on, Janis, cut a little slack and give us a break, will
you. Lighten up!" And I get these pressures and subtle
threats from him. So I'm pretty unpopular with the guys
and I spend a lot of time wondering how long I've got a job.

Janis's position is like Ralph's. No matter what she does, she loses on one front or the other. She must walk a precarious tightrope strung between two superpowers: management and the union. It is a losing situation. She is powerless when it comes to maximizing wins and minimizing negatives.

Marvin, a middle manager, says:

When I hitched on here the company was growing fast. We had the product people wanted and my future was unlimited. I moved up fast. I felt good about what I accomplished. But lately I get a suspicion that some of the others around here are throwing sand in my tanks. I think they're jealous because of how fast I've come up. A couple of the guys on my team drag their heels. They just don't pull their people together and meet their objectives. They don't see how they interface with the others. And I've got to pull it all together. Of course, the boys upstairs, they're looking more at the big picture, and I've got to look through their eyes, too, if I'm to make things work around here. I've been told I've got to be more "seasoned" before I can make the next step up. Well, it's tough to juggle it all. And sometimes I wonder if some of them want to hold me back. Anyway, I've come to a roaring halt here. I've leveled out. You can't stand still, you know. You either go up or you go down. I sure don't want to go down. I want to keep winning.

Marvin faces a multitude of conflicting demands. His position at the middle of the organizational ladder puts him at the crossroads between focused task objectives and broad-range future planning. When he centers on one, the other is neglected. When he attempts to think like the "big boys," those below feel he is not giving proper supervision. When he attempts to work with his team, guiding them on a day-by-day basis, those above feel his vision is myopic and that he needs seasoning. Marvin wants to get ahead. To do so he must satisfy the conflicting demands placed on him. Furthermore, because subordinates see him as overly ambitious at their expense they may retaliate by being uncooperative. So while Marvin seems to have a great deal of power because of his position, he feels like a monkey in the middle, unable to grab the ball and run with it.

CONFLICTING ROLES

A similar dilemma is one of conflicting role demands. This can be a woman executive who is expected to be supermom, superwife, and star employe, or it can be a manager whose company expects him to travel and whose family wants him at home.

Consider Rosie, an attorney:

This morning William, the director, said he has an urgent project and wants me to stay late. I told him that I couldn't work late because my husband and I have tickets for dinner and the theater which we bought over a month ago. My husband's really been looking forward to it. William only said, "Yeah, a typical woman, always putting the family first!" What he said really irritated me but I worry about my job with all of these lay-offs. So I called my husband and explained that I had to work late and wouldn't be able to make the dinner but I hoped to make the play. As you might imagine, he was pretty annoyed and said, "That's typical. Your job always comes first!" I just can't win.

Rosie faces conflicting roles. Her boss expects her, as a highly paid professional, to make personal sacrifices to meet company deadlines. Her husband expects her to put their family plans before the job. Rosie faces mutually exclusive demands. Like the others, Rosie feels powerless. She has little to say about her boss or her husband's expectations; they are imposed upon her. Of course, many men suffer similar conflicts between responsibilities to their families and the demands of their jobs. As men increasingly take on responsibility for raising children, these kinds of conflicts will probably become more common among fathers.

VALUE CONFLICTS

If you work in a sensitive field such as police work, IRS investigation, military, weapons research or nuclear power, you may face value conflicts. You may believe in what you do and strive to do a good job, yet everywhere you go people criticize you for the work you do. You feel misunderstood and respond defensively. Or perhaps you avoid people likely to judge you, such as civilians who don't understand what's involved.

Consider Jeff, a scientist:

I love my work and I'm really excited about some of the developmental projects I'm working on. I feel I'm doing a good thing for the world because I'm contributing to some real scientific breakthroughs. The snag is that the projects I work on cause pollution and this causes me a great deal of conflict. I'm really concerned about ecology and sometimes I get upset about it and think perhaps I should quit and get a job elsewhere. The problem is that this is absolutely the best job I can possibly get. There isn't another lab anywhere where I would have as much freedom and as many challenging projects as I have here. And a lot of the things that I do can be used in other capacities. Yet, I know that toxins are a by-product of my experiments. And it really gets to me sometimes.

Jeff's values conflict with his career objectives. He cannot satisfy one without forfeiting the other. While his win-lose situation may be self-imposed, it is no less frustrating than those experienced by Jane, Ralph, and Janis. Jeff feels powerless because of the way he sees the world and the choices he has made. Personal striving often exacerbate the win-lose situations the world flings at us.

Like these examples, many burnout victims are confronted with situations in which they are pressured to meet several incompatible demands because of damned-if-you-do, damned-if-you-don't situations. The devastating impact of these crazy-making situations on the human

psyche has been well-documented in psychological journals. Win-lose dilemmas make us feel crazy and place a
tremendous drain on motivation. Those caught in such a
situation will eventually stop trying to meet the conflicting
demands, and will become burnout victims.

MEANINGLESSNESS

Not all burnout victims suffer losses and feel themselves a
failure, however. Some come to it through success. They
seem to achieve all the desirable goals. Yet, these bountiful
rewards fail to provide the lasting satisfaction promised to
this existential burnout victim who feels empty, undernour-
ished, and helpless to fill the void. This is an insidious form
of burnout. None of the symptoms are manifested as
warning signals in the early stages. There is only a tiny
nagging inner voice saying, "I am living a meaningless life."

Consider Richard Alpert, the Harvard professor who
became Ram Dass:

*I was at perhaps the highest point of my academic career. I
had just returned from being a visiting professor at the
University of California at Berkeley. . . . I had been assured
of a permanent post that was being held for me at
Harvard. . . . I had research contracts with Yale and
Stanford. In a worldly sense, I was making a great income
and I was the collector of possessions. I had an apartment
in Cambridge that was filled with antiques, and I gave very
charming dinner parties. I had a Mercedes-Benz sedan and
a Triumph 500 CC motorcycle and Cessna 172 airplane and
an MG sports car and a sailboat and a bicycle. I vaca-
tioned in the Caribbean where I did scuba diving. I was
living the way a successful bachelor professor was supposed to live in the world of "he who makes it". . . . Something was wrong. . . . Here I was, sitting with the boys of
the first team. . . . and in the midst of this I felt here were
men and women who, themselves, were not highly evolved
beings. Their own lives were not fulfilled. There was not
enough human beauty, human fulfillment, human contentment. I worked hard and the keys to the kingdom were*

*handed to me. I was being promised all of it. I had felt I
had got into whatever the inner circle meant. . . . But there
was still that horrible awareness that I didn't know
something or other which made it all fall together. And
there was a slight panic in me that I was going to spend
the next forty years not knowing, and that apparently was
par for the course. And in off hours, we played "Go," or
poker, and cracked old jokes. The whole thing was too
empty. . . . I experienced being caught in some kind of a
meaningless game. . . . And in the face of this feeling of
malaise, I ate more, collected more possessions, collected
more appointments and positions and status, more sexual
and alcoholic orgies, and more wildness in my life. . . .*

—Baba Ram Dass

WORK OVERLOAD

Work overload means having more work than we can
perform in a given amount of time. Overloaded people are
harried with too many tasks to do and decisions to make
while constantly behind schedule, worrying about time and
deadlines. Work overload is physically stressful. But work
overload, in and of itself, does not cause burnout as long as
people feel they can control what happens and they receive
adequate wins. You may be very tired, you may be
"stressed out," but your motivation can still remain high. By
contrast, an overload of work that is ambiguous, punitive,
or characterized by the other situations just described is a setup for
burnout.

People overloaded with the
types of work described earlier
are prime candidates for burnout.
An overload of win-lose
situations or impossible
tasks, for example,
compounds the overload
problem and speeds up
burnout.

BUREAUCRACY

Burnout is not the result of personal weakness or some neurotic vulnerability. We are all susceptible. Given the wrong conditions, anyone can burn out. Any time you work in a situation in which you feel you have little or no influence, you risk burning out. The frightening fact is that most jobs constitute such situations. In organizations, controllability is not distributed equally: It is allotted to a few. Yet a feeling of having influence or control over our treatment is necessary for high motivation and peak performance.

We are all susceptible.
Anyone can burn out.

Abraham Zaleznik and his colleagues at the Harvard Graduate Business School investigated this paradox in an analysis of 2,000 high-status workers in three occupational groups: management, staff, and operations. They found that, like power, burnout symptoms were not shared equally. Those in operations had significantly more health problems, emotional distress, and job dissatisfaction. Managers, in contrast, had a consistently lower symptom rate. Digging deeper, they found that operations people reported feeling frustrated by the vague goals and objectives set by supervisors who they viewed as technically ignorant. Ralph, the machinist who's story we heard earlier, is an example. Being technically ignorant, his supervisor, John, presented Ralph with incompatible demands for speed and accuracy. The environment that the operations people described was highly competitive, demanding peak performance and fraught with potential failure.

More than those in the staff or management groups, operations people experienced a great deal of conflict between their jobs and their personal lives. While management also encountered conflict and ambiguity, they reported less frustration than the operations and staff groups. Zaleznik's group theorized that the ability to influence consequences helped minimize the impact of ambiguity and damned-if-you-do, damned-if-you-don't situations. Managers are typically less susceptible to burnout because their decision-making power gives them more influence over their situations, which in turn acts as insulation from the negative aspects of the organization. Having an ability to influence personal power helps prevent burnout.

Middle Managers

Not all managers are equally protected, however. Organizational specialist Robert Kahns and his associates have shown that the middle manager is more susceptible to burnout than managers at other levels. The middle manager is typically caught in a psychic squeeze between the incompatible demands of those above and below and his or her own achievement striving. Marvin, the middle manager who was caught in the middle between thinking like the big boys and dealing with the daily details is an example. Middle managers must learn to tiptoe through a psychologically precarious minefield. One false step can mean a motivational blowout. In a downsizing economy middle management positions are the most likely to be eliminated. Many middle managers feel unemployable, which instills a profound sense of helplessness.

Organizations maximize their survival by minimizing the power of individuals. Powerful individuals can change the organization or leave it, which threatens the organization's existence. Organizations resist change: they strive for stability and predictability. It is the pyramid or bureaucratic structure itself that renders individuals powerless. But as we have seen, powerlessness is toxic to individuals. For individuals, powerlessness demotivates and eventually kills the spirit. Individuals must have power, the capacity to influence what happens to oneself and to make what one wants to happen more likely.

SKILL DEFICIT

The victims described earlier might have been able to prevent burnout if they had more refined defenses. Ann, for example, might have been able to increase her personal power with better communication skills. She didn't know how to draw out Burt's expectations nor how to best communicate with him. Similarly, Gregory needed acknowledgement from his supervisor but he did not make this known. The same holds true for Rick, who was unclear about his job parameters. Had Gregory or Rick developed assertiveness skills, they might have been able to prevent burnout.

How you perceive and think about work is important. Rosie would not have been as susceptible to her boss and husband's barbs had she altered her concept of herself as a woman. Likewise, it was Sara, the defense attorney, and Frank's, the rehab counselor, expectations of themselves and their clients that made their tasks impossible. Improved career decision-making skills might have helped Jeff with his moral conflict over creating pollution and prevented his burnout. On the other hand, Marvin's (the middle manager) survival and advancement could have been maximized by using all of these skills. By increasing personal power through skill building, you can prevent burnout. How to do this is the subject of the remainder of this book.

Chapter Four

Pace Yourself

Self-reverence, self-knowledge, self-control,
These three alone lead to sovereign power.

—Alfred Lord Tennyson

Managing your biocomputer effectively is the first path to personal power. By using basic principles of learning you can build and sustain high motivation and peak performance. Similarly, you can reprogram bad habits that sabotage achieving your goals.

PACE stands for four steps for programming effective skills and deprogramming bad habits. **P—Pinpoint, A—Analyze, C—Change, E—Evaluate.** By following these steps you can pace yourself through your moment by moment encounters with the world. PACE is a guide for shedding old habits and programming new ones.

P—PINPOINT

Pinpointing means narrowing your focus to a very specific behavior. Precision is necessary to change a habit or to program a new one. You need to know exactly what it is that you will change. A statement like social worker Sue's "I'm ineffective, I'm not sensitive to my clients" is too vague. We can't get a handle on such a description. There is no starting point for analysis or change. You need a precise description for the behavior you want to change: Effective when? On what projects? What does effective "look" like? Is it the number of clients processed? The degree of client improvement?

Yes/No Principle

You must be able to stop at any moment and answer with an unambiguous "yes" or "no": *"Is this an instance of the behavior I'm observing?"* If you hesitate or qualify your answer, then the definition needs to be sharpened. A more precise definition of "sensitive" might be "asking feeling questions of clients." Such a definition makes systematic observation easier and more reliable. It also helps Sue, the social worker, to focus in on her concern with her work and performance.

People do not act in isolation; our actions occur within a context. What goes on around you plays a key role in what you do and how you do it. Thus, a pinpointed definition includes the conditions under which the action occurs. Where does it occur? Who and what are around? Sue selected the intake interview as the situation: "Asking feeling questions (the behavior) during intake interviews (the situation)." This may seem like a lot of effort. But pinpointing the target behavior is the cornerstone of a self-change program. The time spent at this stage saves you from muddling along and getting lost in frustration later.

A—ANALYZE

There is a tremendous temptation to rush into a change plan, skipping over the critical step of collecting information and looking for patterns. The objective at this step is to determine how the behavior you want to change is programmed.. Success in a self-change program depends on the thoroughness of the analysis because a strategy for making a change is rooted in it. A sloppy analysis yields an inaccurate picture of what's going on.

It is essential to determine how the behavior functions within the situation. This is accomplished by observing specific interactions with the environment. Remember that it's through encounters with the environment that habits—programs—are formed. We typically think of environments as something "out there," but the environment can be something inside you, which includes what you think, feel, fantasize, and your physical sensations. Like events in the outer world, internal events can prompt us to do certain things or serve as a reward for certain actions.

Keep an Encounter Diary

Being systematic is important. Record encounters with your environments, external and internal, to enable you to step back and objectively review emerging patterns. Data will reveal how the habit you want to change works. An easy way to do this is to keep an "encounter diary" in which you record each occurrence of the behavior in question, and note what happened just before (the prompts) and just after it (the controllers).

Ask the Can-Do Question

This question asks, *"Can I actually perform as I desire? Do I have the skill? Do I know how to carry out the action?"* If the answer is "No, I do not have the skill to act as I wish," the problem is a No-Can-Do behavior. You need to learn skills for carrying out the actions. If, on the other hand, you answer: "Yes, I have the skill to act as I wish but I do not do so," you are looking at a No-Will-Do behavior. Here you are doing too little of what you want to or too much of what you don't want to do.

What stops you from acting or feeling as you want? What does your data reveal? What prompts or events trigger the behavior pattern? Prompts can inhibit the performance you desire as well as trigger unhelpful behaviors that you want to stop doing.

Outcome or what happens after the behavior is another important analysis point. We all seek wins and avoid punishment. Wins promote the winning behavior; whereas punishment inhibits what has been punished. This simple but powerful principle controls most of our activities.

Dysfunctional Patterns

NO OUTCOME:

Your analysis may reveal that there is no outcome for the desired activity. We know that when there is no win for an action we are not inclined to repeat it. If this pattern is controlling the behavior you have targeted for change, providing a win for performance is likely to get you the results you seek.

WIN BEFORE OUTCOME:

Another dysfunctional pattern is one in which the win comes before the behavior is performed. Rather than "If I do X, Then I will win Y" you have "After I win Y, Then I will do X" or a "Then-If" pattern. The problem here is that you are getting wins but they carry little motivational clout. Worse, actually, because the win's power as a motivator is dissipated—extinguished, burned out. Rearranging the contingencies so that the win *follows* the desired action is likely to correct the dysfunctional pattern.

NEGATIVE OUTCOME:

Another common pattern is when the desired behavior is followed by a negative outcome—it is punished. Here the intervention is to replace the punishment with a winning outcome.

OUTCOME & WIN FUSED:

Habits are programmed by *prompts*— what comes before and *controllers*— what comes after them.

Other times you may find that an undesired behavior is fused with a win or positive outcome so that the two can't readily be separated. As much as you might "will" yourself to stop the undesired act, you continue doing it because it is rewarded. Overeating and smoking are good examples. Everyone who has ever been on a diet knows the pleasure of sneaking a forbidden treat and its devastating impact on willpower and the waistline.

ACTION AVOIDS PUNISHMENT

A variation of this pattern is when the undesired behavior wins by avoiding punishment or reducing anxiety (turning off a negative). An example is when you agree with someone to avoid an argument. This is the it-feels-so-good-when-you stop cycle and is much harder to overcome because when you don't stop (i.e., don't engage in the undesired behavior) you get slammed with the punitive result you were avoiding. Yet, through one strategy or another, this is exactly what you must do to free yourself from this vicious cycle of avoidance.

C—CHANGE

When you have a good understanding of how the behavior pattern you want to change is programmed—what triggers it and what perpetuates it; what comes before and what outcomes follow—you are ready to develop a self-change plan for rewriting your behavioral programming.

You determine the best way to go about changing your programming from analysis of the data collected. For example, if a No-Can-Do behavior surfaces, where you don't know how to perform the behavior you desire, learning a new skill is indicated. With a No-Will-Do behavior, in which you have the capability to do what you want but you

don't do it, focus on—what occurs beforehand—the programming that triggers the action or on—what happens
afterwards—the controlling outcomes, or both program
scripts.

Changing Prompt Programs

Prompt are events occurring *before* the target behavior
that set it into motion. These before-programs are altered
by arranging your environment to prompt you to act in
ways that will bring the wins essential for sustaining your
enthusiasm for working.

There are three strategies for changing yourself by
changing prompts. You can avoid the prompt. Here the
undesired behavior wouldn't be triggered. A second strategy is to create a new prompt, one that triggers the
desired behavior. Finally, you can change how you respond
to the prompt. This strategy involves desensitizing yourself
to the prompt, so that you "unlearn" or deprogram your
habitual response.

Changing Control Programs

Events *following* a behavior influence the likelihood of that
behavior occurring again. Controllers cement associations
between the prompt and the behavior. The cementing
quality is the prompt's prediction-ability, meaning how well
the prompt predicts your getting a win or being punished.
When the controller is a positive outcome—something
pleasurable—things associated with that experience can
take on prompting power.

Managing outcomes—events that follow behaviors—is a
key step reengineering behavior programs—habits, both
good and bad. The rule of thumb is to provide a win for
desired, enthusiasm-generating activities, to provide no
outcome, or possibly a negative one, for off-target activities such as procrastinating and goofing off. The programming script is If-Then—If I perform X, then I will win Y.

With this programming principle in mind, analyze the outcomes cementing the burnout behavior program you want to change. Look for a pattern, and compare it to these guiding principles. How does it deviate from this standard? Does it turn off motivation? If so, you'll want to change it.

Timing of Wins

When and how often to arrange for wins is key in rewriting behavior programs. Wins have the strongest impact when they come immediately after the behavior you want to influence. The longer a delay, the weaker the influence. An acknowledgment coming six months after the deed has little motivating power.

How often to give a positive outcome depends on the behavior. In the beginning, give yourself win every time you perform. As the new behavior strengthens, slowly begin weaning yourself from having to get a win every time.

Continuous winning renders you vulnerable.

If you've received continuous positive outcomes and they are abruptly cut off, performing will rapidly stop. In contrast, when the frequency of the win is intermittent the behavior it controls is resistant to burning out. A good example is playing with slot machines. Sometimes a lever pull brings coins; more often it doesn't. Intermittent wins keep us dropping coins and pulling levers.

DEVELOP A WIN MENU

The Win Menu, as the name suggests, is a list of things and activities that are wins for you to choose from. When you have such a list, you can give yourself a win after you've performed in a particular way. Using a Win Menu enables you to tailor rewards to your mood and the moment.

Identify Potential Wins

Do you grant yourself little indulgences throughout the day, such as coffee breaks, an extra fifteen minutes at lunch, or a personal phone call? These indulgences can become positive outcomes simply by placing them after a behavior you want to encourage. Don't take away these privileges; instead make enjoying them contingent (*if* I file ten folders, *then* I get a cup of coffee) on doing what you have decided to do.

For example, Myra, an independent insurance agent, didn't like making out client reports and analysis forms. She often made herself miserable because she let them pile up and then had to sacrifice her precious weekend catching up. This one small part of her job was casting all of her work in a drab shade of gray.

Myra's one pleasure was spending about an hour and a half in the afternoon at a coffee shop reading the paper and sipping expresso. Her coffee-house visits were a pleasure that had potential for being a motivator. She made an agreement with herself: after she completed all the R & A forms for the day, *then* she could go to the coffeehouse. With this small if-then program, Myra put a halt to her procrastinating and she enjoyed her coffee and paper even more. She had tapped the motivating potential of her afternoon pleasure by making it contingent upon finishing the forms.

"If–Then" is a simple but powerful program.

The Win Menu has three categories: (1) What you do a lot, such as getting a cup of coffee, calling a friend, even combing your hair; (2) Activities you like doing, such as reading the paper, going to a movie, walks on the beach, sleeping late, and so forth; and (3) Things you want, such as buying running shoes or a new CD. Wins need have no limits. They can be small or large; material, social, personal, or work activities. A side benefit of using the Win Menu is that creating it helps to clarify what you want. Oddly enough, simply listing what you want increases the chances you will get it.

Remember, burnout is prevented by developing a sense of personal power, which can be accomplished by giving yourself wins when you perform as you want. Not only do you get more wins in your life but you build your feelings of control. This simple formula contains the means for psychological well-being.

Revitalization begins by deliberately arranging to get positive outcomes. You immediately begin getting what you want. This motivation booster fuels forward motion. Personal power is a feeling of being able to influence the world to get what you want. This is the opposite of helplessness.

The key is to make getting what you want contingent upon your taking a small step. Don't worry about how small the step is, as long as it is movement toward the goal.

Goals give you something to shoot for.

Satisfy your wants. Burning out is characterized by a pronounced absence of satisfaction. Turning around burnout is no easy task. It has a negative momentum that requires a great deal of energy to stop.

DEVELOP A CHANGE PLAN

Finally it is time to set forth a plan for change. The plan includes a goal with small steps for reaching it. It specifies what win or reward you'll receive for each step on the way to reaching your goal.

Set a Goal

Goals are important because they give you something to strive for, to aim at. Without a goal you are a ship at sea, without a destination, going around and around, never making headway. Set a reasonable, attainable goal. Many people set themselves up to fail by setting their sights on the unachievable. You can always revamp your goals.

Establish a Baseline

A reliable way to assure a viable goal is to look at how often you are now performing the behavior in question. Count it. If you have already done a good job pinpointing, counting instances of the behavior should be straightforward. You can keep a tally on a file card you carry around. After several days of counting, look at the frequencies. Are you engaging in this activity more than you thought, or less?

How often you are currently performing the behavior is your "baseline." A baseline describes the level at which you are performing before implementing any change plan. The baseline is used as a reference point for evaluating your success. It is the measure with which you compare your performance during and after your change plan. The baseline also gives you a level for establishing your first objective.

Set Small Step Objectives

Objectives are steps on the path, a series of markers toward the goal. The goal is where you want to go; objectives get you there. They guide you in determining what to do or not do in the moment.

Goals are reached by taking many steps and meeting many objectives. An objective is a statement of what you will do to achieve the next step.

Objectives describe what you will do and the situation where you will do it.

When using objectives you know exactly what you will do and when you will do it. For example, Sue, the social worker, wanted to increase her effectiveness by building

---

SMALL STEP OBJECTIVE

I will _____
                          (WHAT)

when _____ for _____
            (SITUATION)   (HOW MUCH)

rapport with the client during intake. Drawing people out with "feeling questions" was one way to accomplish this.

Set the objective for a small change over a short time period.

She pinpointed a feeling question to be a question that asks for another person to communicate feelings, such as "How do you feel about . . . ?" and "Do you feel angry (sad, anxious, good, etc.) about . . ?"

In listening to taped intake interviews, Sue could easily decide if any particular question was a feeling question. Sue, for example, would ask the feeling questions during intake interviews. She might also ask questions that elicit feelings when talking with friends, but these would not be part of her objective.

An objective specifies at what standard you will perform.

An objective states how long, at what level of quality, to what degree, or how many times you will act. The rule of thumb for success is to set the objective for a small improvement over a short time period.

Don't set yourself up to fail by demanding enormous changes. Instead, begin at your current level of performance with the first objective. For example, from data she collected during intake interviews, Sue found she was asking two feeling questions on the average. In her first objective she started with asking two feeling questions during the next two intake interviews. This was an objective that got the ball rolling and Sue knew she could meet.

Begin at your current level of performance.

The feeling of accomplishment in meeting small achievable steps sets a success cycle into motion and will go a long way to bolster you against burnout. Once you've begun your change plan by setting an objective at your current level of performance, then proceed in small steps.

Ask yourself for small improvements only.

For example, Sue's second objective required that she ask at least three feeling questions in the next intake interview. It's similar to practicing yoga. In yoga, you assume a posture that you can do without undo strain, then you stretch just a little bit. You don't demand too much or try to force yourself into a position.

Reward Yourself

Sue looked over her Win Menu and decided that she would buy a particular magazine she wanted as a reward for meeting her first objective. She also decided she would silently acknowledge herself after each feeling question she asked. This immediate positive outcome bridges the gap in time between acting and getting the magazine. Self-acknowledgement has other benefits. Sue paid more attention to feeling questions she and others made during daily conversations as well as in the interviews. This kind of heightened awareness facilitates rapid learning. Also using self-acknowledgement while seeing yourself succeed strengthens its power to motivate you.

YOU MUST ACT

Good intentions alone are not enough to change behavior. Good intentions don't ensure that things will go right. You must act.

The name of the game is action. Doing. Overcoming
your inertia and acting will give you a whole new lease
on being creatively alive. Action is the single most
effective antidote to depression, anxiety, stress, fear,
worry, guilt, and, of course, immobility.
—Wayne Dyer

This brings up the issue of commitment and discipline. To succeed you must have commitment—good intentions and discipline—a way to motivate yourself to carry out your good intentions. One obstacle is the tendency to rebel, which gets in the way of doing what you want. A bigger obstacle is simply not knowing how to manage yourself.

Self-Contract

A simple technique for building commitment and discipline, called a "self-contract," is a written agreement with yourself stating what you will do. A self-contract is something like a New Year's resolution in that you are making a resolve to do something or change in some way. It differs, however, from a New Year's resolution in a few notable ways. First, New Year's resolutions tend to be global statements like, "I will be more receptive to change," or "I

SELF-CONTRACT

I agree to _____
                                (OBJECTIVE)

When I complete this I will _____
                                          (WIN)

_____
CONTRACT TERM

_____   _____
        DATE   SIGNATURE

will lose weight and take care of my health." By comparison, the contract contains a pin-pointed statement of what you are going to do, when and

The road to hell is paved with good intentions.

where you will do it. "I will ride the exercise bike for ten minutes when I get home from work."

The contract describes the win you will give yourself when you meet the objective. New Year's resolutions are rarely stated as contingencies: if I do X, then I'll get Y. The contract has a term or termination date, whereas the resolution is open-ended: "I will stop smoking" as compared to "Today I will not smoke during breakfast."

The open-endedness of the New Year's resolution sets you up to fail.

Most smokers don't stop "cold turkey," which is what the resolution demands. If you go all day and then have a smoke you have failed in your resolution. You learn that you can't do what you decide to do. Your self-esteem and confidence in yourself decline. By contrast, the self-contract teaches you that you can do what you decide to do. You can be without smoking for one day during breakfast. You can successfully do what you determine. Your self-esteem and confidence in yourself grow.

Don't Over-Reach

Make the contract for only as long as you are sure you can stick to it. This might be an hour, a day, or a week. For example, the person riding the exercise bike for ten minutes might write a contract to do so for three days. When the contract term ends, you are free to decide if you want to renew it.

SET YOURSELF UP TO SUCCEED.

Write down the agreement with yourself, your self-contract. This promotes commitment. It's helpful to have a friend, coworker, or mate witness and sign the contract to provide self-imposed peer pressure. It is surprising how effective such a simple technique can be.

E—EVALUATE PROGRESS

Seeing progress toward your goal provides nourishing feedback and promotes continued movement. It feels good to succeed. Sometimes early change is hard to see. Suppose, for example, you wanted to think more positive thoughts and fewer negative ones. And suppose you counted positive and negative thoughts before starting any change program and you were thinking 100 negative thoughts and 25 positive thoughts a day. Suppose in the early stages you reduced your negative thoughts by 20 percent to 80 a day and increased your positive thoughts by 20 percent to 30 a day. A 20 percent change is considered good progress, but without some sort of objective evaluation, it might be hard to see it among 80 negative daily thoughts.

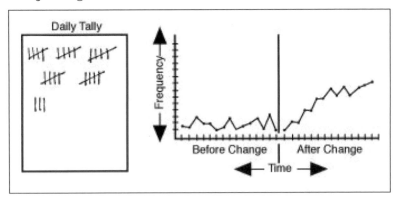

Proof of progress in black and white can help, especially in the beginning. Progress in a self-pacing program is something you can feel good about regardless of the negative factors that exist in your work situation.

Suppose evaluation reveals you haven't made the progress you had hoped. You can take immediate troubleshooting action to tweek your programming script. There is no need to drag an ineffective change plan on for weeks and weeks, becoming discouraged and frustrated. Absence of change isn't a fault or something to feel guilty about; rather, it indicates a need to go back and systematically reexamine each PACE step. Maybe you didn't state the objective clearly so that you didn't know when to do what. Perhaps you demanded too much of yourself. Perhaps some other aspect of the action plan needs revamping. Evaluation is an intricate part of pacing yourself. By focusing on your goal and looking at your progress toward it, you can keep yourself on-target.

When the target behavior is clearly pinpointed it is easy to evaluate your progress.

If the behavior is not clearly pinpointed, it is difficult to evaluate. For example, when Sue, the social worker, said, "I'm not effective," it was difficult for her to establish a baseline. She could not count instances of effectiveness. On the other hand, when she pinpointed effectiveness as asking feeling questions in intake interviews, it was a straightforward matter to count the number of feeling questions and log their frequency on a graph.

Continue counting how often you engage in the behavior after implementing your change plan and compare this to your baseline. The evaluation is a comparison of how often you are performing the behavior now with how often you were performing it before implementing your change plan.

Chapter Five

Manage Stress

*E*vents that stress us are called stressors. Many stressors are universal, such as fear and anxiety. Loud noise, like low-flying airplanes, screaming sirens, and jack-hammering in the street are stressors. Threats to your safety are stressors. Some stressors are learned such as becoming anxious when giving a speech or having to tell someone what to do.

Change is the most ubiquitous stressor. Any change, even change for the better, is stressful. **Change is a stressor.** Change requires adjusting to new conditions. Change is threatening because it brings uncertainty. Loss of control and feeling helpless are stressors. When you can't control situations, circumstances could turn against you.

GENERAL ADAPTATION SYNDROME

Your body carries on certain basic functions, like breathing and blinking, automatically. Such automatic responses make up your "basic operating system." When encountering a stressor, your basic operating system responds with what is called the "general adaptation syndrome," which has three stages: alarm, resistance or adaptation, and exhaustion.

Encountering a stressor rings the **alarm** to activate your physical systems to prepare to fight or flee. The energy demand is tremendous. It requires physiological changes in the adrenal cortex, hormone secretions, heart rate, breathing, and muscle tension, which exact a toll, which we call "stress".

During **adaptation** you resist the stressor while seeking a way to nullify it. Physical activation drops somewhat from the peak reached during alarm, but continues at a moderately high level as you search for ways to influence the world in ways you want. When you succeed in dealing with the stressor, functioning becomes easier and activation drops back to maintenance level.

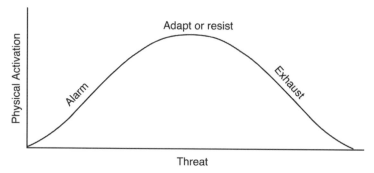

If, on the other hand, the stressor continues unchanged, activation level remains high. Continued physical demands combined with repeated failure to control the situation is experienced first as frustration. If there is no way to turn off the stressor, the frustration turns into futility. Soon comes **exhaustion**, the third stage of the stress response.

Stress and Burnout

Stress is the fever of burnout.

Stress does not cause burnout any more than a fever causes pneumonia. Fever is a symptom, but not the cause of the pneumonia. While getting rid of the fever will not stop the illness, an unchecked fever is serious and can compound the destructiveness of the pneumonia.

So the fever must be treated. You can think of stress as being the "fever" of burnout. Eliminating stress alone is not going to stop burnout. But because stress wears down your physical resistance it needs to be controlled.

KEEP A PERSONAL STRESS LOG

Understanding the relationship between activation level and performance is central to managing stress. Looking at the graph, notice that when activation is low—such as when you're bored or drowsy—quality of performance suffers. Performance also suffers when activation is high, such as when you feel panicky. On the other hand, a moderate level of activation is optimal for peak performance.

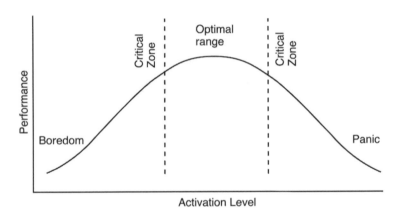

The first step to managing stress is to identify situations that stress you. Then gather information on what prompted the stress and how you respond to it. This process enables you to see your response habits so that you can develop a plan for change.

It is helpful to keep a personal stress log where you keep notes about what stresses you and how you respond. When you feel frustrated, worried, pressured, angry, excited, anxious or upset, stop and rate your distress level, using a scale from 1 to 10, with 1 being "very little distress" and 10 being "extremely upset." Record your rating in your log along with a description of the situation, including who was involved, when and where it happened. Describe your response to the distressing event including what you were thinking, how you felt and what you did.

Look for Patterns

After you've collected data on your stress for several days, review your personal stress log, looking for patterns. What generalizations that you can make about when you experienced distress? What situations, people, times, or days seem to trigger your distress? You might notice that deadlines are a reoccurring theme, or perhaps a person or situation appears several times. Look also for patterns in your responses. Pay particular attention to responses you use over and over. Avoidance patterns are particularly revealing.

Avoidance programs keep you imprisoned.

From this analysis you can fashion a plan for managing your stress responses so that you can prepare for encounters with particular stressors. For example, if you know that speaking with a particular person on the phone upsets you, before calling you might spend a few minutes breathing deeply, while reminding yourself that you are not the target of this person's anger.

LEARN TO SENSE ACTIVATION LEVEL

Learning to sense your level of activation from moment to moment is essential to managing stress. You may believe that you know when you are stressed, but this is often not the case. Most people do not accurately read their activation levels and are not aware of it.

To illustrate, try the Tense-Fit experiment:

Make a very tight fist with your left hand and continue holding it tightly for 60 seconds. Notice what you feel, where you feel it, and how intensely you feel it. While still holding your left hand in the tight fist, make another very tight fist with your right hand and compare the way that your right hand feels with how your left hand feels.

You probably noticed that the strength of the sensations in your left hand dropped as you continued applying tension to the tight fist. That is, when you first made a fist in your left hand the sensation of tension were very strong but it dropped off considerably in only 60 seconds of holding a tight fist. This became evident when you made a fist with your right hand because the sensations were much stronger in the right hand than in the left one. This phenomenon where sensations diminish is called *adaptation.*

Generally, the greater your activation level, the more tense your muscles. However, because sensations of tension can drop off, it is easy to misread tension levels and thereby miss a vital stress warning signal. It's much like driving your car with a broken temperature indicator. You know how serious that can be!

Sensations of tension drop off so that you don't realize that your basic operating system is going full-tilt— you're stressed out!

Biofeedback

Biofeedback is a popular method for sensing activation. A digital device measures an autonomic processes in the body— such as brain waves (EEG), muscle activity (EMG), galvanic skin response (GSR). Through a sound or digital display, you are given feedback on your level of activation and told how it compares to the optimal range.

Biofeedback can increase awareness of what is going on in your basic operating system, but it has a few serious drawbacks. Biofeedback devices can be expensive and to cumbersome to carry with you. Typically the feedback training has a narrow focus, such as devices that measure muscle tension being limited to working with one or two muscles at a time.

A small weather thermometer that is inexpensive and can be carried with you can be used as a biofeedback device. Use a thermometer that indicates decreases as well as increases in temperature. Hold the bulb between your thumb and first finger to read your skin temperature. When activation goes above the optimal level, blood is withdrawn from the hands, feet, nose, and ears to supply the increased demands of your heart, so your skin temperature goes down. If your finger temperature is below 98.6° F, your systems are activated.

Self-Observation

Self-observation is method of sensing activation level that requires no mechanical devices. But first, you must learn to discriminate between sensations of tension and those of relaxation.

The Sensing-Tensing Experiment illustrates how this works:

While *lightly* tensing, make a fist with your left hand. The degree of tension should be *just enough to notice.* For 7-10 seconds objectively and dispassionately study exactly where and how the sensation of tension feels. Next, create contrast in the sensations by *quickly* releasing the tension and consciously relaxing the muscles in your left hand, while objectively watching what you experience in your left hand. In a detached manner, compare how your hand feels when relaxed with how it felt when tense.

Learning to identify tension in your muscles involves systematically tensing and relaxing various muscle groups throughout your body, one at a time, while studying how the sensations feel. The objective is to learn to identify small amounts of tension so that you can then take action to reduce the tension before it gets to an extreme—so that you can bring your activation level back into the optimal range.

HOW TO STUDY TENSION AND RELAXATION

Find a place where you can be comfortable and won't be disturbed for about a half hour. Lie on your bed, couch, or a futon on the floor, or alternatively sit in an overstuffed chair. Kick off your shoes and loosen your belt and any tight clothing.

Tense and relax each muscle in the list of muscle groups below, one at a time, as follows. With eyes closed, tighten the muscle just enough to notice the tension. It is important to learn to detect light tension, so *do not tense tightly*. While holding the tension for about seven seconds (except for the feet—hold these for three seconds), study the physical sensation of tension in the muscle.

Next, *quickly release* the tension from the muscle, relaxing it as much as you can and study the sensation of relaxation for ten or more seconds. Compare the sensation of relaxation and tension. Then tighten the muscle just enough to notice the tension a second time, while studying how and where the tension feels for you. Compare the feeling of tension to the feeling of relaxation. Then quickly release the tension and relax the muscle as much as you can and study the way relaxation feels and compare that feeling to the way that the tension felt.

MUSCLE GROUPS

ARMS AND HANDS

Hand and forearm: Make a fist.

Biceps: Bend the arm at the elbow and make a "he-man" muscle.

FACE AND THROAT

Face: Squint eyes, wrinkle nose, and try to pull your whole face into a point at the center.

Forehead: Knit or raise eyebrows.

Cheeks: While clenching the teeth, pull the corners of your mouth to your ears.

Nose and upper lip: With mouth slightly open, slowly bring upper lip down to lower lip.

Mouth: Bring lips together into a tight point, then press mouth into teeth. Blow out gently to relax.

Mouth: Press the right corner of your mouth into your teeth and push the corner slowly toward the center of your mouth. Repeat for the left corner.

Lips and tongue: With teeth slightly apart press lips together and push tongue into top of mouth.

Chin: With arms crossed over chest, stick out your chin and turn it slowly as far as it will go to the left. Repeat for right side.

Neck: Push your chin into your chest at the same time as pushing your head backward into the back of your chair to create a counter-force.

UPPER BODY

Shoulders: Attempt to touch your ears with your shoulders.

Upper back: Push shoulder blades together and stick out chest.

Chest: Take a deep breath.

Stomach: Pull stomach into spine or push it out.

LOWER BODY

Buttocks: Tighten buttocks and push into chair.

Thighs: Straighten leg and tighten thigh muscles.

Calves: Point toes toward your head.

Toes: Curl your toes.

Make sure to tense only the muscles in the area that you are studying while keeping other muscles relaxed. For example, to tense your biceps you bend your arms at the elbow and make a "he-man" muscle. While doing this let your hands hang limp. If you make a fist at the same time that you tense your biceps, you are tensing two muscle groups rather than one, which makes it harder to study the sensation of tension in the biceps.

Learn to Discriminate

The objective is to discriminate between two feelings—tension and relaxation—so that you can recognize each.

It is something like holding a heavy rock in one hand and a lighter rock in the other and "weighing" the two. Discriminating a very heavy rock from a much lighter one is easy. By comparing the weight of one rock against the other you can learn to identify small differences in weight. You can train yourself to identify small changes in tension by studying the sensations in a tense muscle, then comparing that feeling to how the muscle feels when relaxed.

It takes about twenty minutes to go through your entire body slowly and systematically tensing and relaxing your muscles. You can develop an internal monitor by going through the above-described exercise at least three times a week for two or three weeks. Study the more tension-prone areas, such as muscles in your face or shoulders for five to seven minutes each day. In as short a time as two weeks you will notice you are much more tuned into activation level of your basic operating system. The more you practice, the better your internal monitor will become.

PROGRAMMING THE RELAXATION RESPONSE

Biological processes occurring during relaxation allow the body to repair and prepare for optimal functioning. Personal power increases when you can relax at will. If you can keep activation within the optimal range when faced

with a crisis situation you will remain alert and have all
your resources to draw on to deal with the situation.
Confidence grows as you are able to remain cool regardless of provocation. You feel in command instead of helpless.

Training yourself to relax is a simple process that takes
about three weeks and has two important components.
First, you must learn to identify tension in the muscles.
Without this sensing ability or "internal monitor," you will
not know when to relax. Second, when you have identified
tension, you command the tension to be released.

Develop a Relax Command

Programming a "relax command" can be done at the same
time that you develop your internal monitor. The actual
command word doesn't really matter. It can be any word,
but "relax" is good because it already has the association.
When you're tense other people say, "Hey, George, come
on and relax. Just relax, pal." However, you might want to
use a different word such as "calm down," "quiet," "chill
out," or any word you prefer.

Pair the relax command
with the sensation of
tension release.

After selecting a word to use as a relax command, create a
strong and clear association between the command word
and the physiological sensations of relaxation. The objective is to associate your word with the *feeling of releasing
tension.* As you systematically go through the muscles in
your body, tensing the muscles one at a time.

Think the command word, "Relax,"
just at the moment when you
quickly release tension.

Each time you do this the association between the relax
command and the release of tension becomes stronger.

Thinking the relax command should come just an instant before actually releasing tension. Soon thinking "Relax!", will your basic operating system to release tension—and relax.

Relax at Work

Practice in a quiet spot for about two weeks, then slowly transfer the relaxation training into your daily routine. The key word here is *slowly*. If your first attempt to use the relax command is during a highly charged emotional encounter you are likely to be disappointed in the result because the situation will probably overwhelm the command—and your confidence will drop.

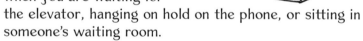

   Instead of a coffee break, you might close your office door, turn off the lights, and spend five minutes practicing the relax command with one or two muscle groups. Or you might practice during times when you are waiting for the elevator, hanging on hold on the phone, or sitting in someone's waiting room.

   Next, use the relax command in mildly tension-producing situations such as riding the bus home from work. This is an ideal way to unwind for the evening. Or try it before making that phone call you have been putting off. ***When you sense tension, take a deep breath, focus your attention on the tense muscle, think the relax command, and consciously release the tension.*** As you notice success, slowly increase the disturbance level of the situations.

BREATHE DEEPLY

Deep breathing is an easy, fast way to reduce stress. You might assume that you breathe correctly. After all, it's natural. However, many people breathe shallowly, which is incorrect because all the air is not forced out of the lungs. If you are breathing correctly your abdomen should go out when you breathe in and go in when you breathe out. You are breathing properly if, when by placing your hand on your abdomen your hand goes out when you inhale and in when you exhale.

Slow, steady, smooth, deep breathing lowers activation level.

Breathing Practice

To develop your ability to breathe deeply, which fosters relaxation so that your body can rest and repair, do this breathing exercise for five to ten minutes each day.

> Breathing exercise:
>
> Start by breathing in slowly for four seconds and hold the breath for four seconds. Next exhale slowly for four seconds and hold your empty lungs for four seconds. As you do this, count the breaths from one to four as follows: 1 (inhale) and 2 (exhale) and 3 (inhale) and 4 (exhale) with "and" coinciding with the hold phases. Then begin again with 1. Focus all your attention on breathing and counting as you breathe in and out slowly.

As you gain skill and lung capacity, slowly increase the time at each phase to six, then eight seconds. When you notice you attention wandering, let the distracting thought go and bring your attention back to the counting. Anytime you notice yourself getting overly excited or feel tense, you can relax with a few minutes of deep breathing.

USE YOUR IMAGINATION

Your imagination can be a powerful stress-management tool. To see how this works, imagine the following scenario. Imagine you are sitting on the grass in a lovely little park that is nicely landscaped and well cared for. You have

Your body responds to the images in your mind as if those images were real. brought a cloth to sit on, a bottle of mineral water, some cheese, bread, and fruit. It is a lovely warm spring day. There are butterflies flying and a couple of bees busily working in the nearby clover flowers. You can smell newly cut grass. Your snack is delicious. *Stop.* Notice how you feel and using a scale from 1 to 10 with 1 being very relaxed and 10 being very tense, rate how you feel after imagining yourself picnicking in the park.

Return to your picnic in the park. Again, imagine enjoying your delicious snack as you luxuriate in the warm spring weather. Suddenly you hear a distant noise. Coming your way is an old pickup truck followed by a large cloud of dust. The truck screams to a halt at the curb near you and eight frolicking teenagers and very two large dogs—a Doberman and a pitbull—jump out from all sides. The dogs run frantically after one another. The kids prop a portable radio blasting heavy metal against a nearby tree and scatter out for frisbee. Excited by the flying frisbees, the dogs yelp as they try to catch them in their snapping jaws. Suddenly a misguided frisbee flies just a few inches over your head. Pursuing the frisbee, the two dogs are running straight toward you. *Stop.* Notice how you feel and using the same scale from 1 to 10, rate your tension level after imagining the noisy scene and the dogs running toward you. Compare this rating with the first one.

If you are like most of us, you felt calm and relaxed when imagining yourself enjoying a delicious picnic. Just imagining the warm sun, the butterflies, and enjoying the cheese and water relaxed you. When the teenagers arrived you probably noticed your muscles tense. Perhaps your heart rate increased and breathing quickened. Seeing the dogs with their teeth coming straight at you probably triggered considerable tension.

What we imagine can be as powerful as what is actually present in the moment.

Your body responded as if you were really in that park and not just imagining it. This is a key to using your imagination to manage stress because you can control activation with what you picture in your mind. By thinking about pleasant calming situations you can reduce your tension level.

Create a Pleasant Scene

Stress can be lowered quite rapidly by taking a few deep breaths and imagining a pleasant scene. It is best to have a well-developed scene to call on rather than to try to ad-lib when a threatening situation is upon you. When a pleasant scene has been well rehearsed, you know exactly what to imagine. A pleasant scene can be anything: a real situation, such as hanging in a hammock in your backyard, or an invented one such as riding on a billowy white cloud. There need be no limits. The only requirement is that imagining it relaxes you.

Stress can be lowered quite rapidly by taking a few deep breaths and imagining a pleasant scene.

Select a situation that you find relaxing for your pleasant scene, review it in your mind and then write down one or two paragraphs describing the fantasy. Describe the setting. Add as much detail as you can about what is there. Think in terms of the five senses. What do you see? Hear? Feel? Smell? Taste? Add these to the description. For example, if your scene is lying on the beach on a warm summer day, you might see

other sunbathers, the sun glistening on water with a sail boat in the distance and fluffy clouds. You might hear the waves lapping the shore and seagulls screeching and feel the warmth of the sun and the blanket under you. You might smell the salty water and taste a cool soda.

The more the scene stimulates your senses the greater its power to relax your body.

After writing the first draft of your pleasant scene, close your eyes, relax by breathing deeply for a couple of minutes, and rehearse your scene. Imagine all the details you wrote on the paper. Bring it to life by making it as vivid as you can. It may be easier to imagine in one "sense" than another. You may be able to hear things in your imagination, but not able to smell anything. People often report that they can imagine situations but can't "see" anything in their imagination. If you can't see anything, then just *imagine* what you would see. Likewise, if you can't smell anything in your imagination, then just imagine what it would smell like if you could smell it. Do the same for the other senses.

Be active in the . Do not look at yourself as a character on a TV screen; instescened *put yourself into the situation.* Imagine yourself inside your body during the fantasy. After imaging your scene for two or three minutes stop and add more detail to the written description of the scenario. What did you find in your scene that you did not write on the paper? Add these to the description.

PRACTICE OFTEN

A good time to work on increasing the power of your fantasy is at the end of the deep-muscle-relaxation-training sessions. When you have systematically relaxed all of your muscles and are deeply relaxed, then bring your fantasy to mind. Project yourself into the situation and make it as vivid as you can. Remember to notice what you experience in each sense. Notice how relaxed you feel. Slowly transfer use to your daily life.

The more often you imagine yourself in the pleasant scene, the more relaxing power the scene will have.

ENGINEER YOUR ENVIRONMENT

Managing stress is not restricted to reducing dangerously high activation. There are times when lethargy or boredom prevails.

Underactivation is stressful and can inhibit performance.

For example, every Friday afternoon Celia must prepare a report containing a lot of figures. It's always a tedious task because she's tired from the week, anxious to move into the weekend, and bored with the repetitive reports—so her activation is way down. She just can't quite find the energy to work on the report. Consequently, she ends up making a lot of errors and doing an inefficient job.

Look again at the figure on page 74 notice that pro-longed high activation will finally give way to exhaustion.

Moderate activation (stress) level is optimal for peak performance.

By increasing the stimulation of her environment Celia can stimulate her activation to bring it up into the optimal range.

When your internal monitor tells you that you are in the high critical range, for example, you can lower your activation and bring yourself back into the optimal range by reducing the stimulation of your environment. Similarly, when you are bored you can increase your activation and move into the optimal range by increasing the stimulation of your environment. Most of us understand this principle intuitively. The problem is that we often use potentially harmful methods of increasing or decreasing activation levels such as taking coffee, alcohol, or drugs.

Music

Most people don't realize that mood can be altered faster with music than with drugs. Try a simple experiment. From your CDs or iPod select an instrumental piece with a simple, repetitive melody and a slow, even beat. Then select a second piece that has a fast, changing beat with a strong percussion emphasis, the more chaotic the better. Next, relax yourself until you feel calm. Play the slow music and notice your internal reactions. How does it feel? What is your activation level? After a minute or two stop the music and relax again. Now play the high-intensity music and notice how you respond. Most likely you noticed a sizable increase in activation in less than a minute when listening to the music with a fast beat.

Music pulls our heart strings. We respond both physically and emotionally. You might feel nostalgia when listening to *Pomp and Circumstance,* like dancing when listening to a disco tune, or maudlin listening to a love song. Celia might increase her efficiency in filling out the tedious report forms if she had a radio in her office and switched it to an upbeat station. The high-intensity music would bring her activation up to the optimal range and the increased alertness would help her perform at her peak. On the other hand, work that requires intense concentration can raise activation to dangerously high. When doing such mental work Celia would do better to turn the dial to a station that plays calming music because low-intensity music lowers activation level.

Color

Soft, muted colors and regular designs have a calming effect. Bright colors such as reds, yellow, oranges, and bold designs in clashing colors are stimulating. Like music, color and design can be used to regulate activation. Jack, for example, was fascinated by abstract paintings, so he put one on a wall in his office. On the other side of his office he placed a painting of a Hawaiian sunset. When he needed to calm down he gazed at the gorgeous Hawaiian sunset; when he needed a boost he looked instead at the abstract.

The color and style of your clothes affects those around you. When I lead stress-management workshops I often wear a dress that is dark blue with a simple Oriental flower on the bosom. Watching the flower with its blue background all day has a calming affect on the participants. On the other hand, in another workshop I might wear a bright red outfit.

Colored Lights

You can't change the decor of your office or home as easily as pulling off a dress—or can you? With the flip of a light switch you can change the intensity of any environment—along with your mood. Compare the affects of a soft-white light to that of a harsh one. What about soft yellow, blue, red? If you've been backstage in a theater you probably noticed banks of colored lights that can be turned on to help create the mood needed for the play.

I discovered quite by chance that I could transform a dreary, depressingly gray day into a bright one simply by wearing glasses with yellow lenses. Having lost my dark-brown tinted sunglasses I dug out my old ski goggles with yellow lenses to protect my eyes while riding my Vespa motorscooter one cold windy March day. Typically, I avoided riding in adverse weather, but I had no choice that day because my car had been stolen and "totaled" by joyriders the night before. I was having a bad day!

Wear yellow lens glasses to feel great on a gloomy day.

Yet, I arrived at my destination feeling lighthearted, unaffected by the chill. I wasn't even depressed about having a wreck for a car. Everything changed, however, when I pulled off the goggles. Not only did the world change back from bright to gray again, but the temperature seemed to drop 15 degrees. With my cheerful mood evicted, I immediately felt victim of an unfair world. After that experience I understood the cliche "looking at the world through rose-colored glasses." Do not underestimate the power of color and light in managing stress. Use it.

People

Of all things in the world, other people, especially strangers, are probably the highest stimulation. Even our closest friends can be unpredictable. A group of people, especially strangers, are extremely stimulating. Without realizing it, you probably use this factor to regulate activation. It is stimulating to go to a party and stand in a crowd of people for entertainment. Other times you might want to "get your head together," so you go on a walk in the woods to avoid people.

I've found when I have tedious, repetitive tasks that just have to be done, I can do them best in a coffeehouse, listening to the music, watching people go by, and drinking coffee. On the other hand, writing that requires intense concentration is best done late at night in the isolation of my office.

Baths

Baths are another age-old method of modulating body tempo. Stretching out in a tepid bath will relax you every time. Alternatively, when you need to be perked up it is best to take a cold shower. If you have trouble getting started in the morning you might take a cold shower first thing. Whereas, if you are tense when you arrive home after work, a warm leisurely bath or a few minutes in a hot tub will probably do the trick.

Food

Food is a powerful regulating tool. Spicy and unusual foods are stimulating, whereas bland and familiar foods like mashed potatoes have the opposite effect. A quick look through an herb and tea book will suggest many alternatives to drugs. Cayenne pepper and ginseng are two natural stimulants; milk and valerian tea are relaxants.

Hunger

A mild degree of hunger is stimulating, whereas after a large meal you probably get drowsy because your basis system activities are devoted to digestion. I used this regulation principle when I first began leading day long workshops. At that time, performing in front of a group of people who may be hostile and would be judging me was overstimulating. I managed my stress by getting up an hour early and treating myself to a large breakfast of eggs, pancakes, and hash browns at a local cafe, while I leisurely reviewed my lesson plan. Then I drove slowly to the workshop site, with plenty of time to set up and relax before the participants arrived. The bulky meal and the sense of control (from having extra time) brought my activation back into the optimal zone so that I could perform at my peak.

As time passed, however, I was no longer nervous when leading workshops. In fact, there were times when the last thing I wanted to do was to get up early in the morning and spend the day teaching. I needed to have my activation increased to perform well. So I traded the long breakfast for an extra hour of sleep. Then, grabbing a slice of toast, a piece of fruit, and a vitamin pack, I left for the session on a nearly empty stomach. The mild hunger was just enough to push me up into the optimal range and the extra rest boosted my stamina.

Exercise

We tend to think the more exercise the better, but this is not necessarily so. Again, when you have been highly stressed all day, vigorous exercise would not be advised. You could exhaust yourself.

Some people get into an exercise regime, sticking to it rigidly without checking their internal monitor to see what they actually need at the moment. It is better to take a reading on yourself and then adjust the intensity of your daily exercise.

On days when you are depressed, a strenuous workout would be advised; on days when you're pressured, light exercise such as a walk around the block will help release tension so you can relax.

Fantasies

Fantasies have unlimited potential for regulating activation. You can imagine real environments as well as the implausible. Use adventuresome or sexual fantasies to perk yourself up, and fantasies about eating a wonderful ten-course meal or your "pleasant scene" to relax.

HOW TO INCREASE STRESS TOLERANCE

Unrelenting activation wears out the body's resources and eventually gives way to the third stage of stress—exhaustion—if you don't act to reduce chronic high activation. You simply can't tolerate it forever. You can, however, increase your stress tolerance level. For example, a sense of being in command, having choices, having fun, and feeling pleasure all increase tolerance—which enables you to withstand higher stress levels, greater threat, and more activation for longer periods of time.

You can tolerate more job pressure and frustrations in situations where you feel in command.

The same is true with pleasure. When you're doing something that feels good or that you consider to be "fun", you can tolerate greater stress. Consider a roller-coaster ride and what you actually feel when you shoot straight down at 60 m.p.h.. This would be a truly terrifying feeling you would never repeat if you

Stress Buffers

Being in command

Having choices

Having fun

Feeling pleasure

Gaining meaning

didn't view it as fun. Sexual intercourse is another example. Here, too, you can withstand higher stimulation. I'm sure you can think of other examples. By contrast, situations in which you feel passive or powerless or experience pain lower stress tolerance.

Over-Stimulation

Have you ever had this experience: Tired from an unusually demanding day, you drink a cup or two of extra strong coffee, hoping it will revive you. Instead, you fall asleep shortly afterward. The caffeine seems to help bring on sleep. How can this be? Are you immune to the stimulant? There is a simpler explanation. Think about what happens when you're on the edge of the high critical zone (see the figures on pages 73-74.) and you consume a

stimulant. The additional boost pushes you into the exhaust phase so both performance and activation drop—
while extracting a physical toll. You experience an activation shutdown caused by stimulation overdose. This
method of regulation is common.

Often used stimulants include coffee, amphetamines,
sugar, nicotine, and vigorous exercise. Without realizing it,
you might be using one or more of these stimulants to
overdose yourself. Sally, for example, did well in her demanding job but there was residual stress. One of her
great loves—and weaknesses—was German chocolate cake.
She fell into the habit of picking up a piece at a neighborhood dessert shop after work. At bedtime she snuggled up
with a book and luxuriated in the rich sweet chocolate. She
always fell to sleep immediately. The sugar in the cake may
have overstimulated her, pushing her into exhaustion—and
sleep.

Chapter Six

Build Skills

R emember when you were a young child, eagerly learning life's basic skills, like how to climb stairs or tie your shoe, cross a busy street or count to twenty-two, and later how to drive a car or dance? Chances are with each feat you felt a little bigger and stronger. Each ability enlarged your horizons and your personal power. You could do more and have more of what you want.

Mastery—doing something well—feels good. You like yourself more and get positive feedback from others. When you feel powerful and approach situations with an I-can-do attitude, difficulties become a chance to exercise your "muscles." By contrast when you lack needed skills, people point to you as an example of the Peter Principle because you appear to have reached your "level of incompetence." Your days are a struggle as you avoid situations that require the skills you lack so you won't look bad. You feel incompetent, incapable, and helpless to change it.

Mastery feels good and is empowering.

Without the appropriate skills you can't succeed in completing tasks required of you. No-can-do becomes no-can-get. Because the future is uncertain having specific skills is less important than knowing how to acquire them when needed. A frequent villain behind burnout is poor problem-solving skills. The burnout victim doesn't know how to pinpoint what is dragging motivation down or how to develop a plan to change it.

IDENTIFY WHAT YOU NEED TO LEARN

While your ultimate goal is to achieve a certain outcome, you get there by focusing on your moment-by-moment behavior. So you must pinpoint what stands between what you are doing now and what you must do to gain the outcomes you seek.

Outcome is the end result you desire; behavior is what you do—the actions achieve the outcome.

For example, completing a report on time is an outcome; making an outline and dictating the report are behaviors that create a completed report.

Review the notes in your Personal Stress Log and the stress patterns you identified in Chapter 5. For each situation and pattern consider what actions you might have taken or what abilities you might have exercised to reduce the distress. Think of how others would have handled the situation more effectively. What skills would he or she would have used. For each situation or pattern, identify the skill you needed to handle the situation well. When finished, review all of the skills you identified. Probably one or two skills came up several times which points to what you need to learn.

Identify the Chain of Behaviors

Typically, a series of behaviors is required to reach the desired outcome. Jeff sells contracts for surfacing driveways and parking lots. Even though he is hard working, conscientious, and puts in long hours, the number of contracts he has landed was way below what he wants. He is frustrated, discouraged, and feels like a failure. Burnout is likely. To halt this vicious cycle Jeff needs to identify the chain of behaviors that lead to a sale.

Behaviors leading to a sale (outcome) interlock like a chain. It's dynamic and moves on its own toward the sale as long as there are no breaks in the flow. To determine the required behaviors and their sequence, Jeff began with the outcome he desired—more signed contracts—and then worked backward, step-by-step, through the required behaviors. The process works like this:

Question: *What specifically must I do to get a signed contract?*

Answer: *I must ask for a signature.*

Question: *What prompts me to ask for a signature?*

Answer: *The prospect's positive enthusiasm: smiling, nodding affirmatively, making positive comments about the deal.*

Question: *What must I do to obtain the prospect's positive enthusiasm?*

Answer: *I must present a persuasive sales pitch.*

Jeff continued with such an inner dialogue until he worked his way back through the entire process of making a sale.

Don't become discouraged if you can't figure out the chain, which is often the case. There are a number of information sources. The best would be for Jeff to observe a high performer making a sale, watching for the behavior chain in action. Find somebody who is successful in achieving your desired outcome. Watch exactly what that person does, step-by-step. You might even take notes.

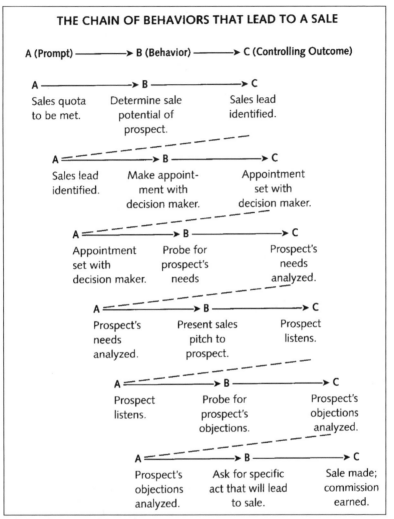

THE CHAIN OF BEHAVIORS THAT LEAD TO A SALE

A (Prompt) ⟶ B (Behavior) ⟶ C (Controlling Outcome)

A ⟶ B ⟶ C
Sales quota to be met. | Determine sale potential of prospect. | Sales lead identified.

A ⟶ B ⟶ C
Sales lead identified. | Make appointment with decision maker. | Appointment set with decision maker.

A ⟶ B ⟶ C
Appointment set with decision maker. | Probe for prospect's needs | Prospect's needs analyzed.

A ⟶ B ⟶ C
Prospect's needs analyzed. | Present sales pitch to prospect. | Prospect listens.

A ⟶ B ⟶ C
Prospect listens. | Probe for prospect's objections. | Prospect's objections analyzed.

A ⟶ B ⟶ C
Prospect's objections analyzed. | Ask for specific act that will lead to sale. | Sale made; commission earned.

LOOK FOR MODELS

A lot of learning takes place through *modeling*—watching other people perform the chain of behaviors. Think about how people learn a sport. The instructor models the skill, like how to swing a tennis racket, then the students attempt to duplicate it. Learning through modeling goes on all the time without our realizing it. When you are new in a job, it's through modeling that you learn "the way we do things around here." You notice what others do that works and soon you're acting in a similar fashion.

CONSULT AN EXPERT

If you can't watch the model, ask the person with the skill to describe each behavior in the sequence. This is what Jeff did. He invited Bill, one of the "star performers," to have a couple of drinks after work. He asked Bill to describe how he sold his customers. Jeff asked questions such as, "Give me an example of what you would say then," or "What did you do next?" or "How did you do that? What did you say?" Jeff's aim was to get specifics about what Bill actually did and when he did it.

CONSULT SELF-HELP BOOKS
ATTEND TRAINING WORKSHOPS

If you are isolated or cutoff from those who have the skills you need, don't despair. There are other ways you can go about identifying the specific behaviors you need to learn. Molly, for example, was a floor supervisor in a candy factory. Being in a position of authority was new to her. She felt unsure and was having a hard time giving assignments and telling people what to do. Simply stated, Molly didn't have "bossing skills." It was a small family-owned company so that the other supervisors were relatives of the owner. Their skills at giving directives weren't much better than Molly's. She was cut off without good models to study. Fortunately for Molly and others caught in the same dilemma, there is bountiful information available.

Self-help books are valuable information sources for behavior chains. Such books break down a process like making decisions or being assertive into "discrete steps." Typically, each behavior in the chain is described with do's and don'ts. Workshops are another excellent source of information. Molly

attended a community-college class I taught on how to
give directives, where she learned the chain of behaviors
involved in giving an effective directive.

Analyze the Breakdown

After you have identified the behavior chain, you must
locate the broken link. Observe yourself carefully, looking
for the step you leave out or don't perform well. Be aware
that it's not always easy to watch yourself when actually
performing. You may get caught up in the situation and
forget to watch.

An alternative is to use your imagination. This is what Jeff did. In his
mind's eye he watched Bill sell a
customer. Then Jeff imagined
himself as he usually handled a
customer looking for behaviors
Bill performed but that he did not.

BE POSITIVE

How you watch is important.
Remember, what you imagine
feels real. Negativity during this pro-
cess is dangerous. In fact, research has shown that we can
learn skills through mental practice. Of course, we all
know this. That's why we mentally rehearse encounters
beforehand. By criticizing and judging your performance,
you implant anxieties and fears that could become insur-
mountable barriers to acquiring the skill. Take care to
avoid doing this.

Be objective, nonjudgmental, and dispassionate. Simply
watch; just observe yourself. Only after you have completed your entire performance and leave your "mental
stage" should you make comparisons with your model. Be
objective when making this comparison, in the same manner as when you compared the sensations of tension and
relaxation in your muscles. Emphasize what you did well. A
nice side-benefit of this self-study is that by remaining
relaxed while watching your not-so-perfect performance,

you can desensitize yourself to "performance anxiety" which frees you to learn the skills you want to acquire.

TEACH YOURSELF A NEW BEHAVIOR

Jeff's situation was pretty straightforward. In comparing his own approach to Bill's he discovered the vital missing link. He wasn't actually asking for the sale. Once he pinpointed this to be the problem, he set an objective to ask the customer for a sale after presenting his pitch during his next call. Signed contracts immediately increased.

Determine a Small Step

Most "no-can-do" problems are usually more complex than this, involving a series of intricate behaviors not being performed. This is what Molly discovered in the giving directives workshop. She found that the language she was using was deferential rather than authoritative. Thus, she needed to learn a new vocabulary and a new way of using it. She also tended to jump into a directive too fast without giving the employee an opportunity to ask questions. For Molly's skill-building to be successful she had to break these complex behaviors down into small steps.

Proceeding slowly is the most effective approach.

Avoid the temptation to try to accomplish too much too soon; instead take small steps. Molly's first small step was to write down what she wanted to say. Then she used the procedure she practiced in the workshop to give a routine directive to Betty Lou, the employee with whom she felt most comfortable. It would have been foolish as her first step to attempt the procedure with Butch who often challenged her.

When sequencing steps make them so easy that you *know* you can perform them.

It doesn't matter how small the step is as long as taking it leads to some improvement or movement toward the end result or final behavior. For example, if you were learning to play tennis you wouldn't start your first practice session attempting a volley with a seasoned player; rather, you would begin practicing your forehand at the backboard. Carry this same principle over into all of your skill-building situations.

Set An Objective

Set a behavior objective for each small step, following the guidelines in Chapter 4. The small step provides the "what" part of the objective. Make sure you decide exactly when you are going to carry out this behavior and how much or how long you will do it. *Make sure to ask only a little of yourself at a time. Require only as much of the new behavior that you feel totally confident you can actually perform*. When you have your objective nailed down you are ready to use your imagination or mental stage to rehearse.

Practice

Relax yourself and then practice the step in your imagination—on your mental stage. It doesn't matter whether you use deep breathing, muscle relaxation, or another technique. What is important is that you are in a state of deep relaxation each time you practice on your mental stage. This deep relaxation is conducive to learning new behaviors.

With all props in place step onto your stage and slowly walk through the behavior specified in your objective. Go in slow motion and focus your attention on the behavior and carrying it out accurately.

Be inside your body and notice how it feels to perform in this manner. Notice all the information coming in through your senses. ***See your behavior work for you.*** Have others in the scene respond as you desire and have your behavior yield the result you are seeking. Focus attention on what you did right during the rehearsal and acknowledge this. Go through this practice several times.

DIRECT YOURSELF

One of the difficulties in learning a complex skill is that we must do so many different things at the same time. Talking yourself through each step helps with coordination. When learning dancing, for example, it's helpful if you count the steps, "two forward, now hop to the right," for example. But that's not dancing. At some point, and very soon, you have to stop talking and dance!

When you mentally rehearse, be both actor and director. While you are performing in slow motion, silently talk yourself through the steps. Direct your expressions, direct your words, direct your feelings. This helps to keep you on track.

Be positive and focus on what you do well. Self criticism while practicing impedes learning. Self-directing helps to block out extraneous thoughts so that you focus all of your attention on the practice. While you are thinking about and following your directions, it is difficult to be worrying and criticizing yourself. Directions need not be restricted to words. You can also direct yourself by "seeing" yourself doing it right.

PRACTICE AT WORK

Continue practicing the small-step behavior on your mental stage while feeling completely relaxed until you feel confident in each action, then transfer practice to your work situation. Don't rush through it. If you set an objective for doing something three times, do it three times. Don't shortchange yourself by carrying out the objective halfway because you'll undermine your own progress and everything will come tumbling down. Build a firm foundation of solid practice.

GIVE YOURSELF WINS

Learning proceeds fastest when the practice is followed by a powerful win. Now is the time to indulge yourself. Each time you enact the small step reward yourself with a pat on the back. Avoid moralizing, telling yourself, "I should be able to . . . and don't really deserve to . . ." This will defeat your learning. Programming a new skill—changing yourself—is not easy. Returning again to the issue of discipline, it's easy to say, "Yes, I will do this for fifteen minutes, three times a day." That's fine and good. But the bottom line is you must do it. There's no way around it. If you don't practice you won't acquire the skill.

Shape Skills

Imagine yourself an sculptor, fashioning a human form. The face would have eyes, nose, and a mouth—but not immediately. To create these you would chisel a rough, round shape for the head, then slowly shape it into finer and finer detail. Follow this shaping principle when acquiring any new skill. Begin with a step that roughly represents the final behavior. Proceed with successive approximations of the skill you ultimately desire. This is important. Employing this principle separates those who succeed from those who try but fail.

Let's look at Hank. He had been told many times that he was cold and distant with coworkers. He felt alienated from the others and was rarely included in any social activities. Through self-observation he saw that most of his conversations were technical and contained a lot of technical jargon. With the aid of a communications workshop and several self-help books, he pinpointed the kinds of questions he asked as the first target of change. Rather than asking his typical fact-eliciting questions, Hank wanted to learn the skill of eliciting feelings. Beginning skill training with his officemate, Gordon, made reaching the first objective easy: "Each day for a week I will ask Gordon at least one feeling question."

After successfully reaching this objective, Hank applied the shaping principle to the how-much component by requiring more feeling questions. His second objective was identical to the first except that he required two feeling questions instead of one each day. Having met this objective he again increased the number of feeling questions he planned to ask Gordon. Next, Hank fine-tuned the "when" portion of the objective. Again, he began working with the person he felt most comfortable with—Gordon—and slowly shaped when he asked feeling questions. When he achieved a high frequency of feeling questions with Gordon, he moved to Rhonda, an attractive woman in the office around whom he felt somewhat uncomfortable. After meeting a series of objectives for asking Rhonda feeling questions, he again increased the difficulty of the situation by moving to Manuel, around whom he almost always felt intimidated.

If you were learning a sport, such as skiing, you'd begin with simple movements. As you mastered the basics you would increase the complexity of the behavior being practiced. The instructor might ask you to ski across the hill while keeping your knees bent and your uphill ski forward. After mastering this step, the next step might be to add a turn at the end of the transverse. By slowly increasing the complexity of the behavior, you would soon be skiing down the slope from side to side.

Find a Practice Lab

Hank wanted to be able to initiate warm, friendly conversations with people he hardly knew, not just with those in
his office. This would be a valuable skill for his business
trips as well as in his social life. To accomplish this goal he
selected Henry's, a neighborhood tavern frequented by
people from his office complex. Henry's was his "practice
lab." In Henry's Hank slowly increased the complexity
(what) of the behavior he was teaching himself. At first
glance this may look like a long, laborious process that
takes time and work. On the other hand, those who have
refined their social skills did so over years and years of
informal training.

Just as you should direct yourself when practicing in
your imagination on your mental stage, it's helpful to self-
direct when practicing in real life. For example, Hank might
think to himself, *"Sit down. Take a deep breath and relax.
Good. Just be calm now. Yes, breathing feels good. Here
comes the waitress. Order a beer. Now look around and see
who's looking my way. Oh, there's someone over there. Just
relax and smile. Be natural. Good, that was easy."* In this
way Hank directed himself through each step.

Self-directing may seem artificial but it helps. Not only
is it easier to stay on target but self-directing also blocks
out destructive negative self-talk. Practicing a new complex skill usually feels unnatural at first. Expect this. Ease
yourself in by talking to yourself. It's okay. But don't be
abrasive like some dictatorial teachers you have suffered.
Direct yourself in a helpful manner. Be positive and guide
yourself gently. Most important, acknowledge what you do
right.

TROUBLESHOOTING

If you're not achieving your objectives there are three
troubleshooting points. First is the **controller**, what happens after the action. Is there a powerful win following the
behavior? A win is needed to reinforce the programming.

Wins encourage you to repeat the behavior again in the future. If you have objectives that require carrying out the behavior a certain number of times and you are missing the target, you may not be supplying a powerful win. When practicing make sure to provide a win each time you carry out the practice step. If you have been providing a win with poor results, then experiment with other wins. Find one that has an impact. Use your Win Menu.

When you don't perform the behavior, look for a **prompt**—what comes before the action. What is there, if anything, to remind you to perform? New behaviors don't come naturally. You must provide an artificial cue, something to prompt you to do it. Then remember to direct yourself through the behavior.

The final troubleshooting point is the **behavior** itself. Perhaps you are requiring a step that's too big. Don't expect to go from practicing your serve at the backboard to playing a hot game with the area pro in one step. Large steps set you up to fail. Build in success by breaking the troublesome step down into smaller steps. Use the shaping principle.

Often you will move rapidly through your objectives in the beginning but have difficulty keeping up the pace.

When you fail to achieve an objective, you have probably required too much of yourself. Go back and reexamine the steps. The best thing to do when you reach a plateau is to slow down and ask much less of yourself—while keeping some momentum going.

Tortoise Rules!
Slow, steady movement succeeds.

The primary reason people have trouble with skill building is that they speed through the steps without doing each one carefully. This impatience is most often at the root of the problem.

EVALUATE PROGRESS

By counting how often the behavior or outcome occurs before, during, and after you implement your change plan, and comparing these frequencies, you can tell if your skill-building program is succeeding. Jeff, for example, could compare the number of sales before and after he began asking for sales. Molly might rate how thoroughly her directives were followed. Hank might count the number of times people in his office seek him out for casual conversation. If your data comparison reveals an improvement in the skill you are working on, then you can conclude your skill-building program is effective.

MAINTAIN YOUR GAINS

Many skills are self-maintaining because the behavior is linked to the reward. Jeff's asking for sales, for example, is maintained by the sales themselves. Molly's using a new style of giving directives is maintained by her employees carrying out the directives. Hank's initiating interactions in social places is maintained by the positive responses he gets. Remember to use the power of your own pats on the back. Self-acknowledgment is something that's always available.

Develop the habit of focusing on what you do well and acknowledging it.

Too often we do just the opposite and dwell on what we do poorly. Such negativity has a dampening effect on learning.

The greater your ability to teach yourself new skills, the greater your personal power. You can't predict what skills the future will demand because the workplace is changing too fast. Now a days job security depends upon knowing how to acquire needed skills.

When you have a method for learning new skills you can take on new situations with less apprehension and a greater sense of control. Even when changes are forced upon you, you will have confidence that you can handle it. This skill-acquisition ability translates directly into  personal power. Other people will quickly sense your power to rise to new challenges and will make more opportunities available to you because they will be confident that you will perform well.

Chapter Seven

Develop Social Support

Supportive relationships nourish us. We are more resilient, accomplish more, and feel worthwhile when we have close supportive relationships. Social support acts as a buffer against stress and burnout. We can tolerate a greater degree of stress when we have supportive relationships. In fact, research shows that people with close emotional and social ties are physically and mentally healthier, spend less time in the hospital, and live longer. A sense of community at work can modulate the stress of both boring and high-pressure jobs. When you've developed solid relationships at work, these can be rallied in times of crisis to help you get over the hump.

Close friends and good relationships with co-workers and family reaffirm your competence and self-worth. Supportive people help you handle difficult situations by listening to your problems and giving feedback. You can turn to this support system for acknowledgement of your efforts and for condolences when things don't work out. They encourage you to tackle challenges, learn new skills, accomplish goals. And friends divert your attention from the negative when you seem stuck to help you develop a new outlook.

Allies can help you get your job done.

It's a rare person who can get a job done without calling upon the cooperation of other people. For one thing, few jobs involve stand-alone activities. Most jobs involve getting input from others in order to do your part. You may be waiting for invoices to be processed so that you can ship orders, for example. Coworkers can help—or hinder—you in accomplishing your objectives. Coworkers can share information you need to perform well; or they can withhold that information, making your job harder. When you have allies who you can count on to help you get things done, you feel more in control—even in very difficult situations. Your personal power grows because you can call on these people to effect certain change.

SOCIAL WORKPLACE

The workplace is a social environment. Succeeding on the job requires more than just accomplishing tasks. Most work is a complicated intermeshing of many activities and functions. We pick up where others have left off, we rely on others for important information. Others must meet their deadlines so that we can meet ours. We work in collaboration in teams, that can come together and disband. We lead; we follow. At every turn we must cultivate cooperation. Success in almost every job means building productive relationships.

Success is rooted in productive relationships.

You can improve your effectiveness at work by taking time to build a network of allies. Allies are not necessarily buddies or people you would pick as personal friends. Allies are people who have some priorities in common with you and can be counted upon to be helpful in certain situations. Allies can give you needed information, connect you with the right person, and open doors to valuable resources. Some alliances spring up naturally. You and someone at the next desk may have certain common problems dealing with a critical supervisor, for example.

We've all seen movies about the private-eye who gets
the low down on the criminal by calling upon a friend in the
police department to run a check on him. The broader your
network of allies, the more opportunities for accomplishment. You will increase your personal power—your ability
to make things happen—by cultivating friendly, helpful
relationships throughout your company, community, and
industry.

Effective people—people who get things done—work through allies.

As management expert Keshavan Nair said, to get things
done it is important to "have friends in low places." These
allies can provide invaluable information about what is
really happening in certain areas of the company. They can
be a valuable conduit of influence. Nurture the alliance and
these allies will increase the chances for success of your
plans and policies because they will convince their peers of
the rightness of your actions.

Allies Build Your Value

People with a network of allies throughout the company
get things done. If you're getting your job done and are an
integral part of helping other people get their jobs done,
you're more valuable to the company. When you're part of
several networks around the office, you become perceived
as indispensable and you'll be viewed as too valuable to
lose when others are laid off. Should your face downsizing
or decide to move on your network of allies is the best
avenue to finding a new job. They will know you are likely
to direct you toward available opportunities.

HOW TO CULTIVATE ALLIES

Allies don't just appear, you must cultivate them. This
requires caring attentiveness to the process. There are
several approaches to making and keeping allies.

Network

Pick potential allies on the basis of the information and resources they have access to rather than their position. Often people in seemingly low positions have useful information. Security officers have information on the comings

and goings of people, for example. Secretaries have information on the preferences of their bosses. Mailroom clerks usually know the cheapest way to ship various things.

Information Is Power

The currency of networking is information. Dr. Bettie Youngs who wrote the book *Is Your Net Working?* draws the analogy with the "old boys" network, "the grapevine," and "the buddy system." She defines networking as a method of making links from the people you know to the people they know. "Hi, Sally Martin suggested I call you. She thought you might be able to give me a referral to a good graphic artist." Youngs likens networking to gardening. Effective networks must be created and cultivated; they don't simply happen. You can't purchase, beg, steal or borrow a network. You must establish your networks yourself and then continuously tend them like a garden. Use networking contacts to exchange information, advice, referrals, and support.

Consider a project you're working on or an objective you wish to meet. What information do you need? What resources? Think of people you know who might have the information or resources or who might know someone who does. Make sure to think broadly about who you know. For example, the clerk in the mailroom might be able to help you get a report out to a client quickly. The butcher at your corner market might be able to refer you to a caterer for a company luncheon.

Communicate Goodwill

People are sensitive to the receptivity of others, especially when first meeting. Your receptivity—the degree to which you respond in a friendly way to approaches from others—is subtly communicated. If you look at the floor when arriving in the morning and go straight to your desk without saying, "Good morning" to coworkers, you've communicated, "If you speak to me I may be unfriendly."

Goodwill is communicated through social rituals. The ones we're most aware of are ritual greetings. "Good morning! How are you this morning?" We all understand that this is a goodwill greeting and not an actual request for information on your well-being. When a person enters a group situation, such as in the example above, or when you walk straight to your desk without saying "Hello" or "Good morning," people wonder "What's bothering her?" or conclude "He's unfriendly."

Communicate goodwill to people around you by using ritual greetings. Make sure that you say "Hi" or "Good morning" in an upbeat voice and communicate friendliness in your nonverbal gestures. The objective is to invite people to speak to you rather than to turn them away. You do this non-verbally, especially by smiling. Eye contact but not staring is important. An open posture, leaning forward, and touching a person's shoulder or arm communicates receptivity. A show of goodwill invites people to speak to you and promotes a comfortable ambiance when interacting with you. It sets the stage for developing a congenial association that could become a beneficial alliance.

Show Interest in Others

The most powerful resource you have for building social relationships is your attention. Keshavan Nair, author of *Beyond Winning,* says that attention to the concerns of others creates obligations. If you want to be a winner, he advises that you show concern for what is important to the people in your organization and they will respond with concern for what is important to you.

Attention is powerful.

When you pay attention to others they feel good about themselves and about you. Showing interest is easy. All you have to do is to ask questions. Find out how others feel about community issues. Ask about hobbies. Be curious about what others want to accomplish.

When asking questions use open-ended questions that draw people out. Open questions begin with words like "what," "where," "how," "when," and "who." A question like "What did you think of it?" shows interest and encourages the person to elaborate upon what was being said. Preferably, questions should be short. The following questions are powerful and versatile. You can ask one in response to most things another person might say.

POWERFUL QUESTIONS FOR SHOWING INTEREST AND GETTING INFORMATION

What happened?

What did you do?

How did you feel?

What's your opinion?

What do you suggest?

What's an example?

What do you mean?

You'll be amazed how many places you can ask these questions and how effective they are in drawing people out and communicating your interest.

Bill: *What a day!*

Bob: *What happened?*

Bill: *Oh, it was crisis management all day.*

Bob: *Yeah? What happened?*

Bill: *This one woman just had a fit over the warranty.*

Bob: *What did she do?*

Bill: *She yelled and threatened and was damned unreasonable.*

Bob: *What did you do?*

Bill: *I listened until she ran out of steam.*

Bob: *Then what happened?*

Bill: *She finally calmed down and I asked her what would correct the situation.*

Bob: *What did she do?*

Bill: *She said I could understand what an inconvenience it was for her.*

Bob: *What did you do?*

Bill: *I told her I understood and that's all it took. She hung up!*

Bob: *How did you feel?*

Bill: *Relief and pride.*

Bob: *What do you mean?*

Bill: *I mean, I felt I did a damned good job with a difficult person.*

Practice asking these simple, but powerful questions. You might write them on a file card that you can carry in your pocket and pull out to review just before you converse with someone. Before you know it, showing interest by asking open questions will become second nature. And you'll be amazed at how having these questions on the tip of your tongue makes it easier to listen and really focus attention on what the other person is saying. You don't get distracted by thinking up your next question. One of the three questions—*"What happened?" "What did you do?"* and *"How did you feel?"*—work in almost all situations. And a second benefit will be the increased quality of information you'll gather. Try it.

Invite Others

Another way to show interest is by including others. At parties and informal gatherings invite others to join your conversation. "Joyce, here, has had some experience with that client too. What do you think his agenda is, Joyce?" Draw people out and set the stage to get attention from others. Help them to open up and feel included.

Don't wait to be invited. Instead take the initiative and invite others to do things with you. Look for small ways to invite others. You can invite a coworker to walk to a meeting with you, for example. Ask coworkers to join you for lunch. Look through the paper for interesting events and ask a friend to accompany you. People love to be invited out.

Be a Teamplayer

Being a teamplayer means working cooperatively to accomplish the group's purpose. This involves passing the ball rather than grabbing it and running for the touchdown yourself. Instead of trying to stand out as the performer, being a teamplayer means setting other people up so they can make the shot. This means thinking beyond your

function and job responsibilities to the goals of the larger group and ways that you can be helpful to others. When another person scores and the team advances because you've passed the ball, everyone wins. You become an important player upon whom others depend.

When you help others accomplish their goals, they are inclined to help you, too. Helping doesn't take a lot of effort. Sometimes it is as easy as sharing information while introducing people to each other. Get outside of yourself and think about what you could do to help someone else succeed. Even if nothing else comes of it, helping feels good.

Pass the ball.
Set others up to win.

When people get caught in the burnout cycle they tend to withdraw and not to have enough energy to extend them-selves to others. They stop giving information; stop being helpful. This in turn closes the person to support of others. Eventually other people withdraw from the person and stop being helpful. A cycle of isolation that sets in.

Give Information

Information is needed to get things done. Be generous with your information. Information is the currency of cultivating allies. Give it freely to people who could benefit from it. If someone performs better as a result of information from you, that person will be inclined to help you when you ask a favor.

INFORMATION IS POWER

Be alert for small ways that you can help people around you to succeed by offering them access to information resources you have. It doesn't take a lot of time or effort. It's more a style of operating, of being generous and outgoing with your information or of being tight and stingy.

Ask for Advice

When you ask others for advice, they are flattered. They feel important and become committed to you. They want to see you succeed. By seeking advice you can identify and clear away barriers and resistance to your projects. Identify who will be affected by your work and what you want to accomplish. Approach these people and ask them what problems and barriers they foresee. Then ask them for advice on handling them. This a powerful method for gaining support and heading problems off at the pass. Not only can you make plans for getting around barriers and correcting problems, but people who may have resisted what you wanted to accomplish become supporters when you seek their feedback and endeavor to find ways to satisfy their concerns.

A production manager could ask advice from the sales manager to get information on what the customers want, for example. Not only is this sort of information invaluable in the production stage, but it is dynamic. The sales staff will be more supportive and committed to selling the product because they were consulted in the formative stages. Additionally, they can show the customers how their concerns were addressed.

Make Others Winners

Making others feel like winners is easy. All you have to do is notice what a person is doing well and comment on it. It only takes a minute. A powerful way of giving credit is to speak positively of something someone did to another person in front of that person. For example, in Janice's presence you might say, "Here's an excellent report on the climatic conditions in the area that Janice prepared for me. The background information is quite thorough and the conclusions are provocative." When you give credit in this manner, not only is the person's self-esteem enhanced, but they become one of your supporters. Additionally, people who've observed you giving credit generally will be predisposed to be positive to you, especially when the person you've given credit to is an ally of theirs.

Consider who has contributed to your work. This may be people on your staff who have performed well. It may be people who have helped by giving you important information. Look for opportunities to acknowledge these people. Take a look at co-workers and other people you interface with. What have they done right? How have they assisted you, even in small ways? Take the time to give people credit for performing. It doesn't have to be a star performance. Give people credit for good performance, for being a teamplayer, for being helpful.

Give credit

Make a list of people who you rely upon to get your work done. For each, identify things they have done well and ways that they have helped you—even if it is part of their job description. Make a point of giving these people credit. While it takes only a few seconds, the potential gains are tremendous. Not only will you gain their cooperation but you help them to beat burnout. Everyone wants to feel that others notice and appreciate their contributions. Be generous with your acknowledgement.

Show Belonging

When you belong to a group or a community, people feel they have something in common with you and feel free to talk with you even though initially they may not know you. The fact that you are a member of the group or club means that you belong and you're "one of us." Belonging implies that you have been accepted.

Actively act in such a way to show that you do belong to this group. Begin by acting "as if" you do belong. Groups usually have certain characteristics or you could call them rituals and styles. These can be in their style of language. People may speak with particular intonations, use slang or speak with a drawl or accent. What they talk about and how they say it may be particular to the group. People may use nicknames, relay stories about group members, tell inside jokes, and use words like "we", "us," or special references like "me and the boys." Sometimes community members wear particular styles of clothing like Brooks Brothers suits, the grunge look, or cowboy style. Sports icons are common. For example, you could show belonging if people in your office are 49er fans and you wear a 49er tee-shirt during the Super Bowl. People in the group may have certain grooming habits like wearing beards or certain hairstyles, for example. There also may be gestures and body language that are common among people in the group.

When you look like you belong it is easier for people to talk with you because you have something in common. Finding ways to show belonging begins by observing people in the group or community you want to belong to. Notice what they talk about. What is the style of dress? What do people do? What do they have in common that identifies them as members of the group? You might keep notes. How can you incorporate language or dress style to show belonging?

DEVELOPMENT A BROAD RELATIONSHIP FOUNDATION

It's important to have supportive relationships at work and to feel belonging rather than alienation. It's equally important to have a broad relationship foundation should one of the main pillars—work or family—show cracks. The hangout is one such cornerstone.

Find a Hangout

People most commonly divide their lives between family and job. There are hidden losses. Parts of you die of attrition, while other facets never have a chance to develop. With all your eggs invested in these two baskets, it doesn't take much to throw both out of kilter. The hangout is a third pillar, a respite from both work and home. Typically some informal spot like an espresso house or a neighborhood-type tavern, the hangout is removed from the cares of the office and home. The TV sitcom "Cheers" is an example of such a hangout. Its story is set in a neighborhood bar where regulars create a sense of community.

The main activity is "hanging out." There are no goals to be met, no statuses to be maintained. You can relax, enjoy a convivial atmosphere, and have an opportunity to meet people of diverse backgrounds. This third place provides an emotional resource vitally important during burnout. You meet people who come together on an equal basis. Hangouts help subdue feelings of alienation and isolation. Regulars can develop a sense of wholeness, belonging, and community. It's a place to gain acknowledgement as a different person—a third person— not a worker, not a spouse.

Separate Home and Work

Many people live in "company ghettos" with all of their friends being from the company and most social activities being company-related. The danger lies in the enormous amount of power the company acquires when you have all of your eggs in one basket. What happens to that basket is very important. You become vulnerable, more susceptible to pressures to conform. There can be far-reaching ramifications seeping into every part of your life until eventually you look like a "company clone." If a problem develops at work, you have a double problem: A threat to your job and the possibility of losing your social support system as well.

There are a number of advantages in keeping your work and personal life separate. With two—or more— support systems, you are stronger. Keeping these two foundations distant from one another forms a more stable base, and provides you with a unique perspective on both.

Sandra's story:

In 1969 I was a teacher in an Army Education Center where almost everyone on staff was an Army person. Having spent my formative years in a military lifestyle, I quickly developed a good rapport with the staff and I liked my job. But, as in any situation, there were subtle pressures to conform. There was an unstated "approved" lifestyle, one that I did not care to live!

At the time that I had this job I lived in a Haight-Ashbury "hippy commune." On the surface the hippy movement endorsed freedom and encouraged doing your own thing. Nothing could have been further from the truth. The same pressures to conform operated among the flower children as everywhere else. There were pressures to conform to certain norms and values—very strong pressures. Some I found compatible, others I didn't.

Each morning I woke up in my hippy commune, climbed into my car, and drove to my other world, the Army base. I felt completely at home and relaxed in both worlds and each insulated me from the other. I remember one day in particular. Another teacher commented, "Sandra, you are so loose, you make me nervous." Ironically, later that day, my boyfriend, who resembled a lion with his mane of long blond hair and thick yellow-red beard, said in irritation, "Sandra, you are so uptight, you squeak."

It was a curious contrast. I knew that each, within their own frame of reference, was absolutely right and I had to agree with them both. But rather than being boxed in by their respective opinions, I was free to choose whichever version of me I wanted at the moment. As my boyfriend berated me for my uptightness, I simply thought back to what the teacher at work had said that morning. Recalling the other teacher's words, I had support, someone to refute my boyfriend's allegation that I squeaked!"

While this double lifestyle doesn't agree with everyone, Sandra found it enabled her to function in a high-pressure situation: the Army. As a side benefit she was able to develop more facets of herself: "I have many more selves and a wide range of available options."

MAKE A PLAN FOR BUILDING SOCIAL SUPPORT

Start building your social support system today. Don't put it off. Make a list of possible things you can do and decide upon one specific action to build your relationship with a friend, family member, co-worker, or in your professional organization. Then make a commitment with yourself to take action.

Start Today.

Write down exactly what you are going to do and when you will do it. And remember to give yourself a "win" for following through. You deserve all the wins you can get. When you have a strong social support system and helpful allies your personal power grows. It is easier to get things done when other people cooperate. Friends and family bring work problems into perspective. Allies expand your sphere of influence and help buffer you from burnout.

Chapter Eight

Tailor the Job to Fit You

When motivation wanes and work becomes a drudgery, you may question why you should tolerate it. Not losing the paycheck may propel you out of bed in the morning and into the commute traffic each day. But in time the arrangement seems less and less equitable. The price is simply too much. The money doesn't compensate for the damage done to your waning spirit. Often weary workers see a bigger paycheck as the solution. But a raise is a short-term high. A week or two later, work feels much the same as it did before. A raise with no other change is probably not going to significantly influence your motivation. Jane, for example, insisted that if she were paid more her job would become more "meaningful." But her focus is shortsighted; she hasn't analyzed the root problem or attempted to make working more satisfying. Chances are, even if Jane does convince her boss that she deserves a raise, she will have the same complaint in a couple of months, perhaps sooner.

Every job has some leeway for tailoring the way it is performed. Generally speaking, changes that result in an increased sense of potency have a beneficial effect on your motivation. Potency is the feeling of "I can do." Following are tactics to consider. With a little from each you might be able to fashion your own best fit.

Tailoring a job is a creative process; there are no pat formulas.

Take time to consider the specifics of your situation. Don't succumb to the urge to seek a salve rather than a solution. Consider the problem in terms of what you can do rather than lamenting over how bad it is and convincing yourself that you are helpless.

TAILOR THE JOB

For many the word "work" calls up images of routinized labor, with the worker going lockstep through the day. This was typical of assembly line work. By contrast, these days many people work in vaguely defined situations with obscure goals. If you're struggling in such a directional vacuum expounding on the failings of the supervisor or the company does little to improve your plight. Not only will this foster a sense of helplessness, it blinds you to a hidden source of personal power.

New professionals just coming out of graduate training programs often find themselves in just such a predicament. The school environment was highly structured with lots of little achievement markers and acknowledgments along the way. Having grown accustomed to such support they are often ill-prepared to work in today's fast moving world. Tucked away and forgotten in a little cubicle, the graduate , feels confused and frustrated with no one to turn to for direction.

Sue, the social worker we met earlier, was just one such person. She was on her own and she eventually realized if she was going to survive working she had to set her own goals and manage herself. This realization was a breakthrough. She no longer viewed ambiguity as a threat but as an opportunity for autonomy. In the process of creating her own structure Sue became less dependent on the external world to fuel her motivation.

IDENTIFY HOW YOU FIT IN

It's easy to wonder how pecking away diligently at your work has impact on anything at all. One way to find out is to identify how you fit into the larger organizational picture. Here's how: Begin by looking at your organization as a total entity and ask the question, "What is the organization's essential output or goal?" In Sue's case, the agency's ultimate goal was to meet client emergency needs by providing food, shelter, and counseling. Proceed backward from the organization's overall output to departmental outputs and then from departmental outputs to your output.

ANALYZE HOW YOUR DAILY ACTIVITIES FIT INTO THE ORGANIZATIONAL GOALS

Organizational Goals

Departmental Goals

Your Output Goals

Chains of Behavior

Behavioral Objectives

SET GOALS

Sue's unit purpose was directing the client to the appropriate service group within the agency. Sue contributed to this larger purpose by providing a description of the client's problem. Once she identified her output, she began working on unrooting the behavior chains needed to make an accurate description of the nature and scope of the client problem. One link in the chain was to establish rapport with the client so they he or she would be more comfortable in discussing problems.

Having identified establishing rapport as a vital link to her ultimate output, Sue proceeded to pinpoint the specific behaviors involved. One of these was to ask "feeling questions." Sue established a personal skill building program for increasing the number of feeling questions she asked during each intake interview.

Goal setting is an essential skill for surviving an unresponsive environment

The goal tells you which way to shoot. By comparing your last shot to the goal you generate feedback. Feedback is the longitude and latitude of where you stand relative to your goal. Because it is a reflection of your progress, the feedback has personal meaning. Even a boring job can be made meaningful by working toward a goal. Once you know how to use it, goal setting is an eternal source of personal power that can never be taken from you. By combining goal setting and self-acknowledgment, you can sustain motivation.

ACKNOWLEDGE YOURSELF

You have an inexhaustible source of powerful wins because you can give yourself acknowledgment and rewards. Unfortu- nately, few of us use self-acknowledgment so that this self-renewing source of power remains dormant. Most people engage in negative-talk instead, which is punitive, and remain dependent on acknowledgment from others.

Self-acknowledgment is particularly important in unresponsive and hostile environments. By acknowledging to yourself your progress towards a goal, you can sustain your motivation—even in the face of criticism.

MANAGE TASKS

Another powerful win is the opportunity to engage in an activity you enjoy. For example, as a child your mother knew you loved math puzzles and hated practicing violin. She may have said "When you finish practicing the violin, you can work on your math project." Because you liked working on math, the opportunity to do so is a kind of reward for practicing the violin. We all understand this principle and use it intuitively to manage others.

Opportunity to engage in an activity you prefer is motivating.

Research has demonstrated that the opportunity to engage in a "preferred activity" can be used as a reward for completing an "unpreferred activity." For   example, when you walk into your office in the morning suppose you are most likely to open your mail and least likely to dictate a report. Opening mail would be considered a preferred activity while dictating a report is an unpreferred one.

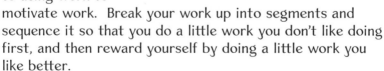

Within this principle lies a key to using work to motivate work. Break your work up into segments and sequence it so that you do a little work you don't like doing first, and then reward yourself by doing a little work you like better.

Let's look at how Gina employed this strategy. She hated filing and consequently left it to last. She did do a little filing each day, but the number of papers she grudgingly stuck in folders did not compare to what accumulated in the "To Be Filed" basket. Gina dreaded filing, yet knew she had to do it.

Using task management, Gina identified photocopying as an activity she liked doing more—"preferred activity". Although the photocopying itself was rather boring, it provided a break in the routine and an opportunity to chat with whomever happened to be in the production room. So she tended to do photocopying right away. Gina made an agreement with herself to do a specific amount of filing before she did any photocopying. The desire to get through the filing and onto the photocopying provided the motivation to file. By managing tasks, Gina worked more efficiently and was less vulnerable to the boring and routine aspects of her work. Her focus switched from dreading to accomplishing. A secondary gain was an increase in personal power as she overcame a burdensome chore.

Campbell also used this strategy. Continuing his professional growth meant he had to keep abreast of the latest developments. But it was becoming increasingly difficult for him to do what he called "later work"—which was work that had no immediate payoff but was important at some later time. He was not keeping up with the stacks of journals and was feeling deprived and unhappy about it. This discontentment was creating quite a problem for him. He felt trapped in what he called "now work"—processing papers, writing routine reports, and sitting in meetings. His day was consumed in satisfying the immediate demands of his job. While he met these daily demands and deadlines with ease, he had less and less time for his "later work" such as going to professional conferences, reading journal articles, working on proposals for new projects, or creative contemplations.

Campbell solved this problem with task management. He set up a schedule that made working on one daily project (a "now" activity) contingent upon doing a little "later" work. For example, he required that he spend 20 minutes reading one journal article *before* he could work on a particular "now" report. Although it was a step removed, the deadline attached to the "now" work provided a deadline for doing the "later" work as well. With this formula Campbell reclaimed the energy dissipated in the numbing routine of now work.

MANAGE TIME

The constant phone interruptions also challenged Campbell's patience. All one had to do was dial his number to get an immediate audience with him, whether he liked it or not. No sooner would he get into a task than the phone would ring again. To create a block of free time from the phone Campbell had to manage time. He told his secretary to hold all his calls between 9 and 11. At ll he returned the calls. Campbell was able to concentrate on one task at a time without distraction. He produced more and did it effectively because he had more production time.

Ralph had a similar problem grasping elusive time. What began as a little harmless chitchat with his officemate had escalated into time-gobbling rap sessions. He wasn't getting anything done. Ralph and his officemate worked out the following plan: Two hours in the morning, from 9 to 11, and an hour in the afternoon, from 2 to 4, were designated as "quiet time." During these periods they agreed to be quiet. If either were restless and wanted to talk, he would go elsewhere for a responsive ear. At the end of the hour they shared coffee and conversation. Managing time created time, Ralph got a lot more done, and he enjoyed his officemate and the breaks more, too.

Set Priorities

It is easy to fall into the trap of working on the next thing that comes by, which is sometimes called "crisis management" rather than working on what's really important to accomplishing your job. By setting priorities and sticking to them you can be more effective. Setting priorities is particularly important when you have too much work and too little time in which to do it. The reality is that there will be many times when you simply must leave certain things undone. This is okay and most employers will accept it so long as you get the important things done and what you don't do is unimportant to accomplishing your major purpose.

It is easy to spend all of your time doing routine things and then find that all of your time has been used up before you get to things that are important. Chances are that the really important things you must do are also more difficult. So it is easy to procrastinate and then find you don't have time to get to them. Setting priorities can help you to keep your eye on the ball and to get the important parts of your job done.

You Were Hired to Solve a Problem

Jobs are created because the organization has a problem. For example, Wynett and James ran a mail-order business out of their home. In the beginning they did all of the work themselves, but as the business grew various problems cropped up. The phones rang so frequently that they could not take all the calls and still process the orders. The number of orders increased to the point that they could not process them quickly enough themselves. Delayed orders resulted in customer complaints. The volume of phone calls and orders were "problems". So James and Wynett created a "job" of answering the phone and pro-cessing orders to solve this problem.

You were not hired to do a job.

Identify Your Purpose

When you identify the problem that you were hired to solve you uncover your purpose. Sometimes it is obvious as in the example of the mail order business. Other times it will be more difficult. One way to identify the problem you were hired to solve is to imagine what would happen if no one were dealing with the problem. Imagine what would happen if the problem simply went unsolved. Focus on the problem to be solved and not the tasks that you or others carry out in order to solve the problem. For example, what is the problem that a receptionist in a law office is hired to solve? Answering phones can be handled with voice mail a lot cheaper than paying for a full-time receptionist. A big problem for attorneys is that people walk into their office unannounced while they are with clients. The receptionist solves this problem by greeting clients, which sets a professional tone, and, more importantly, by keeping them in the waiting area until the attorney calls for them.

The problem you were hired to solve is *your* purpose.

When you've identified the core problem or problems you are hired to solve you have identified your purpose in the company. When you know your purpose, which is the problem you have been hired to solve, then you know what you are to accomplish and can set priorities. Activities that have a big impact upon solving the problem are more important and should have a higher priority than those that have a lesser impact.

Identify Tasks and Activities

List your tasks and activities at work. If you have difficulty remembering them, close your eyes and see yourself at your work space doing what you do while working. Alternatively, for several days jot down things you do as you come to them during your work day. Make sure that you include everything you do, such as answering the phone, completing forms, meeting with coworkers, and so forth.

Rate Impact

Using a scale from 1 to 10, with 0 being "no impact" and 10 being "great impact," rate the impact that each activity has upon your solving the problem you were hired to solve.

Assign Priorities

Use the impact ratings to assign priorities to each task or activity. Assign an "A" priority for tasks and activities with impact ratings over 7; "B" priority for impact ratings from 4 to 6; and "C" priority for impact ratings below 3.

Schedule Activities

Use your priority ratings to schedule your day. Start with "A" tasks and activities. Schedule them directly on your calendar. Leave "C" priorities until last and, whenever possible, delegate them. Consider what would happen if you simply did not do the "C" activities at all. If the consequences are minimal, you might consider dropping the activity from your workload. In many cases you can do this without asking permission. After all, when you've analyzed your purpose and are accomplishing that purpose you are doing your job. If questioned, you have a solid rationale for having dropped the activity.

ALTER JOB FOCUS

Few jobs are clearly defined. While this can be a problem, it is also an opportunity. Take advantage of its ambiguity and shape the job according to what you enjoy doing and what best capitalizes on your skills and interests. First, look around for needs and ways you can provide a service. When you see a problem within your department, write it down, mull it over, and consider how you can convert it into an opportunity. Always focus on this question: "How can I provide a service?"

LOOK FOR A NEED TO FILL

Simultaneously review all of your activities. There must be some you enjoy more than others. Expand and make more important those parts of your job you enjoy most. You can accomplish this by simply spending more time on these parts. When you discover a service you can provide by engaging in an activity you enjoy, grab it!

Make the services you provide visible. Be alert to ways of highlighting what you do—the needs you fill. In this way you can mold the job into one that is more interesting. It will evolve with you, and you'll receive more acknowledgment for your efforts because you have pointed them out. Don't wait passively for the world to notice what you're doing. Most people are so caught up in their own activities that they simply don't see you. Wave a flag; toot your horn.

EXPAND YOUR JOB

Jobs are not static, they are elastic and change. Jobs are alive and can be stretched. They grow and evolve. The best way to expand your job is to take possession of "unattached problems." These are problems that have not been assigned to any specific person. Since these problems are not assigned and don't fall within anyone's domain, they are free for you to take.

Take possession of unattached problems you can solve and that interest you.

In most cases this strategy doesn't require asking permission and you can obtain formal authorization after the fact. Depending upon how important the problem is to the company, you might be able to use it to obtain an upgraded job title, add support staff or services, or possibly even to get a raise.

In rapidly changing environments unattached problems are plentiful. This is true of both expanding and down-sizing companies. Keep a list of the unattached problems you discover. When you have several such problems, consider each, one at a time, and ask the following two questions. First, "Can I solve this problem?" If you can answer yes, this problem is a candidate for you to assume. The second question is "Does solving this problem interest me?" If it interests you and you can solve the problem, then you seriously consider taking on the problem as yours.

Years ago when I worked as a social worker in the San Francisco County Men's Jail I used this principle to expand my job in ways that I found more satisfying. I met with inmates in the jail twice a week to discuss their plans and how I could assist in helping solve their various problems, which included retrieving possessions from hotels, writing pleading letters to judges, arranging for a room after their release, getting meal tickets from social services, providing a razor in order to shave before a job interview, and so on.

There was no central referral service or hot line for these people. Consequently, I often had to research the available services, which took a lot of time. I discovered that services were often referred to in newspaper articles and announcements. So each morning I skimmed the local papers. When I noticed a service that might be useful, I wrote the details on a file card. Soon I had a rather large file of resources. I felt much more competent when a recently released inmate came to my office and I could flip through my files to a service that might help him. Instead of feeling helpless and frustrated when facing the serious problems that the men brought to me, I felt powerful. I had something to offer him.

Soon a curious thing happened. Service providers in other agencies heard through the grapevine about my resource file and began calling me for referrals. In talking with these people, I realized that there were service providers in several agencies working with the same client population. The problem was that we were all disconnected and reinventing the wheel. So I took the initiative and invited several of these people to my office to discuss how we could work together. The meeting was helpful so we began meeting monthly. I never asked my supervisor for permission to keep a referral file or to meet with the other service providers. It was an unattached problem and I grabbed it and ran with it.

Eventually, I moved on to another job elsewhere. Guess what? Maintaining the referral file and holding the meetings were presented as part of the defined job to the new case worker. By taking on an unattached problem, I had expanded the job.

INCREASE DIVERSITY

Variety—working on tasks that vary—can refuel energy. Many people find that when they do the same thing over and over that they lose interest in it. Without interest it becomes difficult to perform well, so quality declines. Diversity can renew interest, even when the various tasks taken individually may each be rather routine.

Despecialize

One way to increase diversity is to despecialize, to become more of a generalist. A generalist does a variety of jobs rather than specializing in one. No matter what your job or station in life there are always ways to despecialize. Antonio, for example, was a research consultant specializing in statistical analysis. While he found it fascinating, it didn't satisfy him. It wasn't enough. Having been through several phases of indifference, he knew his lack of interest was a danger signal. Then the yardman who maintained Antonio's rental units quit. Antonio had to fill in until he could find someone reliable. Halfway through repairing and painting a picket fence, Antonio sensed that a feeling of aliveness was returning. From that point on Antonio spent a little time each week building fences, planting roses, clipping hedges, and spraying bugs. By "despecializing" he found a balance between his mental and physical needs. Doing one or the other of his tasks provided not just an escape but also nourishment.

Murphy, a big city cop, is another example. His idealism had motivated him to join the force two years earlier. He was a compassionate man who felt for others and believed he could alleviate some human suffering through police work. But most of his encounters with citizens were in negative circumstances. They were criminals (or suspected criminals) and he was the bearer of bad news. Murphy felt himself hardening. His idealism was dimming and his compassion becoming dull. He began to despair.

While he still felt police work was right for him, he recognized he had to have some balance if he were to continue. So he took a weekend job delivering flowers. His encounters with people during deliveries were very different from those when on the beat. Now he was the bearer of beauty. Even when the situation was a sorrowful one, his arrival was associated with sympathy and remembrance. His positive image of himself—as well as his confidence in his fellow human beings—was reaffirmed.

Here's how Sue, the social worker, despecialized. Doing intake interviews almost exclusively was becoming an emotional drain. The clients were blending together and Sue felt herself getting dull. Over lunch she discovered that Ruth, the woman who handled client processing, was also experiencing what Sue called "sameness drain." Ruth was bleary-eyed from paper work, and Sue was drained from people work. They laughed over the image of waiting for clients to glide by their desks on a conveyor belt. The idea of trading jobs once a week seemed worth a try. They didn't race into the plan immediately. Over many lunches and dinners, Ruth and Sue tutored one another. Both felt good about the results—a close friendship, a broader skill base, and renewed enthusiasm.

WORK PART-TIME

Part-timing is another way to create diversity. Most week days Matthew was the lunch cook in an uptown restaurant. His evenings were divided between working in a bookstore with a coffee shop serving cake and cappuccino in the early evenings, and later working as a waiter in a singles bar until midnight. Any one of these jobs would have become tedious, but the diversity of the three-way combo maintained his interest. All told Matthew worked about 40 hours a week, made about the same amount of money as if he had worked a full-time job, and had a schedule that allowed him a three-day weekend every week.

PURSUE HOBBIES

Traditionally hobbies have served the purpose of refueling creativity and enthusiasm. The hobby—or avocation— provides an outlet for expression of those selves that are ignored at work. Pursuing a hobby takes you into worlds far away from work. You meet new people, different people. It reminds you that your work situation is not the whole world. Also, as you excel in your hobby you get acknowledgment from others that can help ward off "appreciation starvation" experienced at work.

A hobby can evolve into a new vocation.

Roy was in the training department of a large West Coast police department. He often entertained others in the department and the rookies during training with his cartoon caricatures. His pen won him popularity and livened up many boring classes. One day a witness to a particularly grisly crime shook his head to all the mugshots. A talented artist was needed to translate the victim's vague remembrance into an image. Because of the nature of the crime, the police department didn't want to risk any leakage to the press by using the newspaper's artist. Roy's drawing was accurate, the criminal was apprehended, and Roy had taken his first step to becoming a nationally acclaimed police artist.

SPEAK UP

When contemplating the possibilities of a more dramatic job overhaul keep in mind that your relationship with the organization is contractual. You have agreed to perform a certain service in exchange for a specified amount of pay and benefits. But aside from the salary, length of work-week, the extent of benefits, and general tasks not much else is actually specified in most work contracts. As with any contract, unstated issues are open to interpretation and negotiation by both parties. Too many people give their employers more than they have contracted, so work contracts need to be periodically clarified and renegoti-ated.

No person or company remains static: People change, companies change. What may have been a good arrange-ment two years ago may no longer be optimal. It might be necessary for you to talk with your supervisor about what's dampening your motivation and suggest steps that could turn it around. This requires self-confidence and assertiveness. Don't just dump a bunch of vague complaints

on your boss. Putting him or her on the defensive is not a winning approach. But more importantly, by expecting your boss to solve the problem, you proclaim your-self helpless. It would be better to pinpoint the problem by describ-ing what is happening to your work spirit and suggest possible solutions.

Keep in mind that one of your boss's major job functions is to get work done through people. Constructive speaking up is not the same as complaining or confronting; it is giving the supervisor valuable feedback. It's important for both you and the organization that you speak up and do so effectively. Suffering in silence leads to a loss for both of you. If you feel hesitant or uncomfortable doing this, you may need a skill-building program to help develop your assertiveness skills.

SET LIMITS

Unchecked, jobs can get out of control, creeping into every corner of your life, demanding more and more from you. Forgotten is the work contract. Sometimes it's because of continual crises; other times it's a succession of critical projects; or perhaps even an overzealous supervisor who believes that working late each night is a sign of motivation and, hence, promoteability.

Know your limits. What are the limits of your obligations and responsibilities? Have you agreed to these extras in the work contract? What are your needs outside of work for other activities? When you have answered these and other questions, it becomes time to make your limits known. This doesn't have to be a confrontation. But it is important to speak up and let your supervisor know you have fulfilled your obligations and you have other needs and responsibilities. Explain that when you work more, the organization gets less. Once you have set your limits, keep them.

REDISTRIBUTE JOB RESPONSIBILITIES

Like people, jobs evolve. Consider Clem. He hopped into the saddle of a university computer center and did a superb job of picking up the pieces from the chaos left by his predecessor. He also unveiled an unusual talent for motivating people in the process. Consequently his programs were a success and the center expanded. Demand for computer services mushroomed, and without realizing it Clem's job was mushrooming, too. His responsibilities had multiplied enormously until he could no longer juggle all the projects and departments under his direction.

Overlooking the possibility that his job had outgrown what anyone could realistically manage, Clem felt like a failure. As he saw it, the only solution was to bow out before anyone realized he'd lost his touch. Clem told the residing dean he planned to resign. Fortunately for Clem and the center, the dean convinced him to delay acting until a compensation specialist could take a close look at his responsibilities. Upper management was startled when the analyst recommended three full-time jobs be carved out of Clem's responsibilities.

TAKE A SABBATICAL

A sabbatical, or leave of absence, from your responsibilities to assume a dramatically different one has been a tradition in academia and is becoming more common in the corporate world as well. It is a half-step between staying in your job and getting a new one. You can take on different responsibilities, sometimes in a different part of the country, for an extended period of time, and return at the end of the sabbatical period to your former position.

In larger corporations, with all their levels and divisions, sabbaticals are a feasible solution to the recharging of drained motivational batteries. Sabbaticals have the added advantage of providing a vehicle for expanding employees' capabilities, a big plus for the company and the employees. If you are an "essential component," many companies will consider granting you a leave of absence if they think they can eventually get you back.

This was a tactic Ron used. He had been branch manager of a savings-and-loan company for over five years. Under his leadership his branch outperformed the others on almost every index. But the job was getting to him. On his forty-sixth birthday he was keenly aware of the passing of his youth. Age itself was not a concern, but he was disturbed by his increasing awareness of "paths not taken." Whether it was a mid-life crisis or something else, Ron didn't know. He did know he needed a change and a dramatic one. It was either quit or take a leave of absence. The organization opted for the leave of absence. They hoped to keep him on board until his retirement.

Ron, knowing that his old position was on hold, did something he always wanted to do. He became a kindergarten teacher in a troubled inner-city school. While the other teachers seemed overwhelmed with despair, for Ron

the challenge was invigorating. Ron's enthusiasm
was contagious and
many of the teachers
began to show flick-
ers of life. Rejuve-
nated, Ron returned
to his post at the
savings and loan. He
had a new perspective
on the economic prob-
lems faced by the inner-
city residents and was
determined to seek a
solution. The savings
and loan reaped a
double gain: They used

Ron's leave of absence to train a manager for a new branch
and retained a star performers.

FIT THE JOB TO YOU

Virtually every job has some leeway to tailor it to fit the
person doing the work. Often routines of the job are
shaped more by the last person doing it than by the actual
task. Yet, people forget that jobs are malleable and implement the job in the same style as the last person. When
that style doesn't fit, it is like trying to squeeze the round
peg into the square hole.

A job that doesn't fit can be abrasive
to your motivation.

Don't try to turn yourself into a pretzel. Instead, tailor the
job to fit you. In the process you will increase your personal power because you will feel in command of your work
and you will probably do a better job.

Chapter Nine

Change Jobs

No amount of modification can force a "good fit" with certain jobs. After enough saddle sores you may decide the only way to save your spirit is to get out—an option burnout victims contemplate with longing and fear. The decision is toughest when your job has benefits like prestige, a big salary, or country-club membership. But the real question is: How much is it actually costing to stay in a poorly fitting job? How many of your precious moments are you spending to have the privilege of sitting around the club pool?

How did you get on your current path? Who picked it for you? Answers like "I don't know" or "It just happened" suggest you've complacently followed whatever path you found before you. Passive decision making leaves you ill-prepared to confront the challenge of burnout. Feeling helpless, hope that a good path can be found falters. In this weakened

spiritual condition the burnout victim faces what could be the most important challenge of his or her life: finding a path with a heart.

DOES THE PATH HAVE A GOOD HEART?

Does the path have a good heart?
If it does, the path is good.
If it doesn't, it is of no use.

Both paths lead nowhere;
but one has a heart, the other doesn't.

One makes for a joyful journey; as long as
you follow it, you are one with it.
The other will make you curse your life.

One makes you strong;
the other weakens you.

—Don Juan
The Teachings of Don Juan

FIND A PATH WITH A HEART

The successful quest begins with self-knowledge—who you are and who you want to become. So many of your moments are spent working. Encounters in these moments shape whom you become. How often have you heard, "Hi, I'm John. I'm a butcher (baker, candlestick-maker). What do you do?" Don't deceive yourself into believing you can separate your work from your life. You cannot.

Job Fit

When there is a good "fit" between you and your job— which includes the company, coworkers and so forth—you are more likely to like what you are doing and to be successful at it. A good fit means that what you are doing and the company philosophy are compatible with your basic values. When you resonate in this way with your job, coworkers tend to go the extra mile to help you. Succeeding is easy. Working is usually fun because you like what you are doing and the people you're doing it with.

Many people do not have a good job fit, however. They may not have rapport with others in the workplace. Perhaps their values and lifestyles differ too much. When people see you as different from themselves, they tend to hold back so that it is harder to get the cooperation and information you need to perform well. If you don't like the work, then working is a chore. When you are in a job that doesn't fit you well, it is easy to get into a vicious cycle of poor performance. People tend to withhold, making it harder for you to perform. When you perform less well, then your self-confidence suffers, which sets you up to have even more difficulties performing.

Values

"Values" is a catchall phrase for those things you feel are worthwhile. Values are what really matter; what gives you meaning. Values come from the heart because they have to do with how you feel about things. When work engages your values, you have a sense of meaning and feel you're doing something important and worthwhile. In contrast, work that involves doing things you don't care about leaves you feeling empty. Worse yet is work that violates your values. The path with a heart is the path that engages your values. Everyone is not the same and people don't value the same things. A path that has a heart for me, may leave you feeling empty. So the first step in finding a good fit is to clarify your values.

Values are what really matter; what give you meaning.

One way to uncover values is to examine things you love doing. Get a piece of paper and quickly write down fifteen or twenty things you love doing. Do this quickly so that you tap into feelings and stay away from what you think you "should" or "shouldn't" love doing.

Read over the list of activities you like doing and check the five or six things you love doing the most. Imagine doing one of the things you love doing most and ask yourself, "What do I love about this?" Of the answer, ask yourself again, "What do I *really* love about this?" Keep probing each answer. For example, Ralph loved riding his bike with friends. An onlooker might assume that physical exercise is what Ralph loved. But when he asked, "What do I love about this?" he answered, "Striving toward a goal with friends." Asking what he loved about this, Ralph answered, "The feeling of esprit de corps."

Continue probing until you get to the root value. For Ralph, it might be taking on a challenge with a team, for example. Repeat this exercise with the other activities that you love doing the most. Then question the other activities you love doing.

Make sure to jot down notes from each answer. After you've gone through the process with several things that you love doing, review the notes looking for patterns. These patterns will provide a picture of what is important to you.

FIND YOUR IDEAL JOB

There is an old saying: If you don't know where you want to go, you probably won't get there. The same is true in your work. If you don't know what a good fitting job would be, then you probably won't find it. If you're going to get a job you love you must determine what it would be. One way to go about identifying a good fitting job is to begin with what it is *not*. Identify situations in your current job that bother you. From these bothersome situations you can extrapolate the conditions that would exist in your ideal job.

Identify Bothersome Situations

Close your eyes and recall a typical day at work. Review it in your mind and notice what situations made you feel frustrated or helpless. List these on a piece of paper. Next, bring to mind a particularly distressing day and identify what about it was bothersome. Add these situations to the list. The more specific you are in describing bothersome situations, the better. Turn back to "What Is the Burnout Potential of Your Job?" (page 35) and list each item you rated as a 6 or higher.

LOOK FOR BOTHERSOME PATTERNS

After you have identified several bothersome situations, read over the list several times. Group the bothersome aspect of each situation into categories. For example, problems with management might include lack of rewards, vague directions, favoritism, or criticism. Difficulties with co-workers could include conflicts, politicking, cliques, rejection or taking credit for your work. Problems with the type of work could include writing reports, too much detail, long hours at the computer, or highly technical material. Another category could be environmental problems such as noise, poor lighting, crowded, or fast-paced.

Create a Picture of Your Ideal Job

Mentally review one of the patterns you identified and study the bothersome aspect of the situation. Next, envision a work situation in which this pattern did not occur. What specific ways would the job be different? Play around with it in your imagination until you find an alternative you like. This is an "ideal scenario." Repeat the exercise with each bothersome pattern. Write a brief description of the ideal scenarios next to the respective bothersome patterns.

ENVISION YOUR IDEAL JOB

After you've studied each bothersome situation and imagined alternative scenarios you are ready to make a first stab at creating a picture of your ideal job. Imagine a work situation that includes several of the ideal scenarios you identified. Try to actually see the ideal work place. What is the environment like? Is it inside or outside? What sounds are there? What is the light like? How many other people work there? What are coworkers like? Do you socialize with them? Where? Doing what? Do you have a boss? What is his or her supervisory style? What do you do? What are your work hours like? How do you get to and from work? What do you do in your spare time? What rewards do you get in this job? How do other people treat you? The more complete the picture of your ideal job, the better.

Write a description of the job you pictured. Add as many details as you can imagine. Picture yourself in your ideal job again. Notice what you missed, then add these details to the description. Don't try to do this in one sitting. Begin with the sketch. Project yourself into the ideal job. Notice how it feels. Add details. See the situation, the other people involved, and what you are doing. Edit as much as you like. Continue shaping the sketch until you fashion an "ideal job." This may require many sessions. Come back to it periodically over a week or two—or more. Keep adding features to the picture of your ideal job. This is not a onetime process. Just as you change, so will your ideal job.

Identify Barriers to Your Ideal Job

What keeps you from being in your ideal job right now? Look carefully at this and be specific. On a new piece of paper create two columns. Write "Barriers" at the top of one column and "Challenges" at the top of the second column. Under "Barriers" list everything standing between where you are now and your ideal job.

Taking the barriers one at a time, determine what you must do to remove the barrier and write this in the "Challenges" column. Don't be "realistic." Just write down what it would take to get around the barrier. Pay particular attention to what you are thinking as you do this exercise. If you hear yourself saying a lot of reasons why you "can't," then list "negative thinking" as one of the barriers.

Overcoming negative thinking is one of the greatest barriers.

You can move toward your ideal job but don't expect to reach it immediately. Choose a challenge and make a plan of action for meeting the challenge. Then lay out small steps for getting there. Make sure that you give yourself "wins" for successful steps. Each day you will be a little closer to your ideal job. As you overcome the barriers, you will feel more in control of your work and your life because each day you will be taking action to prevent burnout.

Identify Alternative Jobs

When considering a job change, most people simply head for the want ads in the newspaper or make an appointment with a headhunter. This is not the most fruitful approach. The competition for advertised jobs is fantastic. Big-city newspapers have thousands of readers. More importantly, it is unlikely that a listed job will be uniquely suited to you, or match to your ideal job. Accepting a mass-advertised job means you must fit yourself into its mold. There is a strong possibility that it will not be a good fit. Seek a mold that fits you. Better yet, create your own.

Open yourself to all possibilities. Broaden your vision.

Now that you have a pretty good image of the ideal job you are seeking, it is time to begin a broad sweep of possibilities. Don't restrict yourself to any particular field or allow stereotypes and biases to narrow the scope of your investigation. Look around and see what's actually out there. Save being critical and narrowing down options until you know what's possible. You may believe you know all that is available; but new fields and specialties are born all the time.

People are at work everywhere. Select anyone at all and project yourself into this person. Compare what you discover to the blueprint for your ideal job. People love to talk about their work—just ask. As they paint a picture, project yourself into it. See yourself doing what they do and notice how it feels—how it fits you.

When a field beckons, follow it. Find out everything you can about it. Talk to anyone who knows anything about it. Ask if you can visit their office, plant, or studio to see what they do. Don't be shy. Most people enjoy such show-and-tell. Go to the library and ask the reference librarian to direct you to the occupational directories that describe thousands of jobs along with their future projections, skills, training required, and working conditions.

Follow your bliss.

It's curious how people resist looking into the future in a purposeful way. Deprived of the power of foresight they plod along the path—perhaps disgruntled, perhaps complacent—exercising little control, remaining vulnerable. With this approach finding your ideal job is chancy at best.

Joel is a good example.

We met shortly after he started with the county as a public defender. Over a three-year period I watched Joel sink into disillusionment. Each time we spoke he related a horror story worse than before. Listening to Joel recount the latest outrage during a chance meeting in the stacks of a local bookstore, it became obvious he was beginning to seriously doubt that justice existed; yet he was complacent, entertaining no alternatives, making no plans.

*Unable to resist, I asked what strategy he planned for
getting out. He looked at me blankly. Joel simply did not
think that way. When I prompted him a bit, attempting to
discover his secret dream, he relayed all the reasons why it
wasn't possible to think about it at this time. It would take
two more years to pay off his college loans. Of course,
there was a good retirement plan, and who could match
the pay? He reminded me that for six months he had
worked part time in a private law firm that hadn't worked
out—so that possibility was exhausted.*

*"Certainly," I thought, "there must be a secret dream." I
persisted. Joel claimed there was none. It was as if using
his imagination was taboo unless the action pictured would
immediately manifest. If he had to stay in his job until he
paid off his loans, then there was imagining alternatives
until then. But how much of Joel's spirit would remain in
two years? And what of his health, his idealism, and his
concern for his clients?*

Sometimes people resist because of attachment to
what they have been doing. They literally cannot imagine
themselves doing anything different and refuse to even try.
I have seen people on a meager path who never look down
the other fork of the road, never wonder what might be
around the bend, never even see
another path because they are
gazing steadily at their feet. If the
path you are on is heartless, then it
behooves you to take a look around
and see where else you could be.

HOW TO TRANSFER SKILLS

Many people set aside their dream of
getting into something else because they
think they will have to abandon their
specialty and step back into the pool of
unskilled labor. They are blind to the
possibility that their skills may be transferable. When you analyze your skills with

the objective of seeing how they can be transferred, more often than not you'll find that retraining is not necessary.

Consider Gil's example:

Gil had been an engineer for over fifteen years. He loved his work but he had difficulty working with the other engineers. "The work was fine but I had a group of people involved in their own games. They couldn't or wouldn't communicate. It was hell. I was constantly coming up against a brick wall. Finally, it got to the point where I couldn't take it anymore. I was burned out. I quit, dropped out of life, and became a hermit for eight months. Eventually I realized no matter how far into the mountains I went people would still find me, so I came out of the mountains."

Subsequently Gil became involved in political activity and through a group of friends he ended up volunteering his services at Legal Aid. "I discovered I could still use my skills. As a scientist I solved problems. Once I got over being attached to my identity as a scientist, I saw that I could apply these same skills to legal problems." Then a crisis arose. The agency needed a legal assistant to do research and prepare cases for the attorneys. The crisis paid off for Gil. He stepped into the job and stayed there for four years. Then he set up a free-lance consulting practice specializing in legal research and eventually developed a large clientele of lawyers. He never went back to school, never took a single law course.

What Gil's example illustrates is that most skills are transferable. Both scientists and lawyers must solve problems. Skills such as being able to write clearly, communicate effectively, deliver a persuasive presentation, and solve problems are transferable to a wide range of fields. Often the barrier is only in your mind. Gil advises: "When you make a change like this, the best thing to do is to pretend you've gone to a foreign country, a new culture. Recognize that all the rules have changed. What you used to do or used to be doesn't matter here. Assess what it is that you can do; then look around and find a need for it. " This is good advice.

Analyze Your Transferable Skills

Probably the skills you use in your current job can be transferred to a variety of careers. But don't expect a prospective employer to do the translating for you. You must take the time before approaching an employer to analyze your skills and how they might be transferred.

Make a list of your skills. Sometimes it is easier to start with the technical skills, like ability to repair a particular kind of equipment or run a particular machine. Then focus on your "soft" skills, like ability to make decisions, ability to analyze problems, ability to argue a point, and so forth. Make sure to include your people skills such as ability to draw people out, ability to make people feel comfortable, ability to get others' cooperation, and so forth. Don't forget basic skills like ability to read, to drive a car, and write a letter.

Really push yourself to list what you can do.

Too often people list five to eight skills, mostly technical, and then insist that that is all that they can do. Nonsense! When you take the time to think about it you'll discover that you have dozens of useful skills. In fact, just this exercise of listing your skills is empowering when you stop to take a real look at all of the things that *you can do*.

Next comes the challenging step. One by one brainstorm how you might be able to employ each skill in the field under consideration. For example, a social worker might transfer "counseling" into "job interviewing" and "facilitating employee behavior change". A lawyer might translate "writing briefs" into "analytical writing" or "ability to write concise reports." It's helpful to ask someone versed in the field you are considering to go over your skills and suggest ways that they can be transferred.

Research

Eventually you'll must get out of your imagination and into the world. When you've drawn a pretty good blueprint of your ideal job, it's time to look for real possibilities.

Find the person who has the power to hire you for your ideal job.

If the job doesn't exist, then you must find the person who can create it. Skeptical? Don't be. This is not as hard as it seems. Even if you don't know who this person is or where to look (which is probably the case), he or she can be tracked down rather rapidly.

A study of how people network revealed that the average number of acquaintance links between you and any other person in the United States is 5.5. In other words, you'll need a referral chain of approximately five to six people to locate your man (or woman). Joe refers you to Sam, then Sam refers you to Cheryl, which would be a two-link referral chain. If you're restricting your search to your current locale, the number of links will probably be fewer than five. It's a small world, and you're closer to the person who can hire you for your ideal job than you realize.

The first referral is to be found among acquaintances. Think of everyone you know and identify those people who might know someone who knows the person you seek. If you ever wanted to be a detective or an investigative reporter, now's your chance. Call these friends, explain what you are doing, describe your ideal job, and ask if they know someone who might be able to help you. If they do—and someone will probably have some kind of lead—get a name and ask if you can say they suggested you call. Very soon you will be meeting with a person who can hire you for your ideal job. Most people know someone and are happy to give you his or her name. People feel good when they can be helpful, especially when it's as easy as giving you a name. In addition to immediate acquaintances, you can make initial contacts at the "watering hole". People hang out with others in their profession or from their company. Locate these enclaves. They can be bars or tennis courts, health spas or private clubs.

Association directories, available in most libraries, are another source of leads. Research these and then call up the person who is likely to be the decision-maker. Explain that you are not looking for a job but are researching the available alternatives to make a decision later on and request an appointment. More often than not you will get it. If not, ask for a referral. You will almost always get a referral because people don't like to say no. If someone must say no, it is easier if they can give you something. When you get a referral, call number two and say number one suggested you call. After a couple of calls you'll usually get an appointment.

There are several important things on the agenda for this meeting. First, check the match between what your contact says is available (or possible) and the blueprint for your ideal job. Be assertive and probe. Ask your host if you can go on a tour or speak with other employees. If possible, purchase a beverage in the cafeteria and linger there. Notice the ambiance. How does it compare to what you want? Keep all your receptors open. Notice what it feels like to be in this place. Ask questions. Gather as much information as you can.

If this work environment looks like a potentially good fit, then move to your sec-   ond objective: Uncover the
"hook." How can you
hook this guy or gal?
What need does he
or she have that
you can fulfill?
What service can
you offer?

TOP
BANANA

**Look for problems
you can solve**

People are hired to solve a problem. It doesn't have to be huge problem like balancing the company budget. Make sure it's a problem for the decision-maker—the person who has the power to hire you. Get into his or her shoes and look for manageable problems you can solve. Again, before leaving the interview make sure to get at least one referral. Send a thank-you note. (You might consider sending the secretary who helped you get the interview a thank-you note, too. This could be helpful in the future.) Through this process of interviewing and asking for a referral you will rapidly zero in on the very job you are seeking.

It's not at all uncommon during field research to receive a job offer. But it is not advisable, however, to accept the offer immediately. Don't be foolish and rush through the exploratory stage. Resist grabbing the first offer. Better to indicate that you will seriously consider the offer when you get to the point of making a decision. In the process your attractiveness is likely to go up. The allure of hard-to-get is not restricted to lovers, you know.

Decide

Implicit in having to choose one alternative over the other is the threat of losing. Your basic operating system is non-discriminating when it comes to threats. As soon as a threat is detected, the fight-flight or stress response is triggered and your systems go on alert. Often people handle decision stress by procrastinating, pushing the decision off onto somebody else, or other means of avoidance. Expect a tendency to avoid. It's natural but not conducive to making a good decision.

Good decisions require tolerating a certain degree of stress: thinking about potential losses, being uncertain, and possibly confused. You must be able to go through the stress and come out the other side rather than avoiding it by making a snap decision, or just passively accepting what's given to you. Using the relaxation techniques discussed in Chapter 5 will help you manage the stress your decision generates.

CONSIDERATIONS

The first step in weighing the alternatives is to identify all the considerations of which there are two types: actual changes and opinions. Changes include income adjustments, moving, differences in the work itself, new schedules, and so forth. Opinions are feelings about the changes.

Make sure to consider how the changes will impact others.

Neglecting to consider how your decision will influence important others—family, friends, colleagues—and their feelings about it, leaves you vulnerable. They may sabotage you or pressure you into reversing your decision. Avoid this by listing all the ways your decision will mean changes for other people touched by what you do.

Don't weigh the considerations intellectually; instead, use your imagination once again. For each consideration, project yourself into the future and pretend the change is reality. For example, suppose one alternative requires moving to a different area. Imagine actually being in that new place. *See yourself* living in this new community, making it as real as possible. Include the weather and other environmental factors. Visualize your workspace and doing the things you would be doing. Notice exactly how you respond. What do you feel and think? How do you feel about the weather? For example, do you suddenly realize that long winter months mean being housebound, a lot of snow shoveling, and difficult driving? How do you respond to this?

Reflect on what you observed. Decide if your response is positive or negative and rate the strength of your reaction. Was shoveling snow mildly negative or extremely negative? Did you enjoy the stinging feeling of the cold snow flakes on your cheeks? Go through this process for each item on the list. Don't try to remember your ratings; write them down for later.

BALANCING ALTERNATIVES

It's easiest to compare only two alternatives at once. The objective is to determine which alternative has the largest number of gains and the smallest number of losses. Do this by simply laying the alternatives side by side and taking a look. Sometimes one alternative will completely outweigh the other, making the decision between the two easy; other times it will be much harder. You may have to recycle through the consideration stage a few times. When you finally select one as most advantageous, repeat the balancing process with all possible pairs among your alternatives.

STRESS INOCULATION

Any alternative you choose will involve some losses—often coming before the gains are realized. For example, you may decide to leave the company in favor of becoming an independent consultant. Being a consultant may promise a number of positive gains, but leaving the company is a dramatic cut in income and a lot of apprehension. You have to be able to go through this period of loss to get to the gains.

CHANGE IS STRESSFUL.

Change forces you to adapt, to develop a new routine. Sometimes it's only a minor disruption and adjustment; other times it may be more encompassing. In some cases the stress may be so extreme that you make a quick reversal in your decision or to take some other foolish action. Of course, you want to prevent this.

Stress inoculation is helpful in handling inevitable losses. It works much like a vaccination. The doctor injects you with weakened germ cells, then your body responds to this physical threat by developing antibodies to ward off the hostile invaders. These antibodies are then on hand and ready for any similar future toxic invasion. Stress inoculation is similar.

By exposing yourself briefly in your imagination to the stressful situation, you will be more able to cope with it when the actual situation occurs.

In your mind's eye, project yourself to a time when you would be experiencing the loss. See yourself in the negative situation. For example, if you had to move to a new community, *see yourself* feeling alone and isolated on a weekend without friends. Allow yourself to experience the negative emotions that accompany this lonely weekend. You will probably feel your tension level increasing as the fight-flight kicks in. Just allow yourself to experience how it feels for a few minutes.

EXPERIENCE THE NEGATIVE EMOTIONS.

The next step is important: After you have rehearsed the loss and experienced the increased stress, *see yourself taking some action to handle the problem. Notice as you take the coping action that your tension level goes down.* Try out each coping plan in your imagination until you find the one that works best.

When you have developed your "coping fantasy," inoculate yourself periodically by imagining yourself in the loss situation, enacting your plan to cope with the distress, while noticing your stress level reducing. By using this procedure you will be prepared—you will experience a lesser degree of stress when you are in the real situation and you will know what actions to take. You to feel in command, which will further reduce your stress level. With this simple procedure you'll have increased your personal power and be able to perform more effectively.

MAKE A PLAN AND ACT

Write down everything standing between where you are now and reaching the goal you have decided upon. For each item on the list determine whether or not it is under your control to change it. Examine each barrier and challenge the assessment that you cannot change it. For example, after working as a lunch cook for about a year James decided he wanted to go to chef school to become a professional chef but he lamented that the tuition alone was $15,000. "How can I get that money? I barely make ends meet as it is. I can't save." His friend challenged James's limitation. "Look, James, you're trained as an electronics technician. I know you don't like the work but it pays—and good. If you really wanted to get that money all you'd have to do is to work for one year building motherboards and you have $15,000 and more!" But James did not want to hear this because he equated difficulty with impossibility. Thinking in terms of the impossible leaves you helpless. Instead, think in terms of the possible and don't worry about the probable.

If you are determined and committed to what you want, you have a good chance of getting it.

Determine the minimum change necessary to achieve the goal you have settled on. Go back to the list you made of your skills. Take these skills and rearrange them in every combination you can conjure up to draw a map from where you are now to where you want to be. Be careful of the tendency to shave down the goal, to make it "more realistic."

Consider Dr. Joyce Brothers:

Early in her career, Dr. Joyce Brothers was living on a student's income with her then medical-resident husband and young child. She reports that at the time her husband was earning $50 a month and she earned nothing. Her passionate desire was to have enough money to buy a Cadillac. She decided she would work to get one. At the time the television quiz show "The $64,000 Question" was all the rage. She and her husband analyzed each contestant on the show to uncover the formula for being selected as a contestant. She then used this formula to make herself *into an attractive candidate. She became an expert on boxing, which was incongruous with being a petite blond psychologist. She says, "I ate, drank, and slept boxing. I even borrowed a series of films on the great fights of the century and rented a projector so that I could run them at home." She had her doubts but persisted. Ultimately not only was she selected to be on the show, but won the big prize! A highly improbable way of getting a Cadillac!*

Brothers says this about the effort: "This was a watershed experience for me, the first time I had gone all out, giving up everything else in my life to get what I wanted. And it changed the whole direction of my life. I knew what it was to work and work hard, but I had never worked so intensely before, never had this kind of total commitment. I had pushed my energies and my brain and my emotions to the limit, to the point where it hurt—and it paid off."

Make a Map for Reaching Your Goal

Use your imagination and don't limit yourself. Instead of saying "I can't do that", ask "How can I do that?" Consider every way that you can achieve what you want. Look at your skills you and then make a plan. When you have made a plan and have determined your path it's time to go to work. Many people will go all out for a job, yet when it comes to themselves and their own goals, they work halfheartedly or procrastinate instead. You owe it to yourself to give it your best shot. Chances are you'll hit the bull's eye. The hard part is not the reaching, but the deciding what to reach for. All that is required to get where you want to go is hard work and determination. Remember this: You could be working just as hard for something you don't want.

Instead of saying "I can't do that", ask "*How* can I do that?"

Of course, there will be a price you must pay. Any change requires giving up something. If you have done a good job balancing your alternatives you should know what the price is. Use the stress-inoculation procedure until you can see yourself paying the price without feeling anxious and uptight. Then pay the price and get it out of the way as soon as you can. The important thing is to get on your path and move toward your goal.

INTERVIEWS

Any time you go to an interview make sure you meet with the decision-maker, the person who has the power to hire you. Otherwise it is a waste of time. Personnel departments typically cannot hire; their function is to screen out—to reject. Avoid them. Get to the decision-maker. Your objective is to persuade this person that you want the job and to show that you can do it

Unroot the decision-maker's problem.

Don't concern yourself with the larger company's need. Instead, look for a service you can provide to the decision-maker. Look for a problem that needs solving; then demonstrate that *you* can do it. Forget about the limitations of whether or not a job exists. If it doesn't, the decision-maker can create it. In other words, if you have unrooted a genuine problem that needs solving you might be able to invent your own job. This is ideal because when no vacancy exists you have no competition. Whether there is an actual job existing already or you're proposing one, you need to demonstrate your ability to do it.

RESUMES

Most people were taught in high school to prepare a resume that lists work experience from the most recent backward in time. This form is convenient for the system, but it is neither the only nor the best form to use to present yourself because it highlights gaps in your work history and can obscure what you actually have to offer. And it's dull. You don't stand out.

The purpose of the resume is to get you an interview.

You don't need to have all the dates you ever worked and other specifics written down. If the decision-maker is interested, he or she can get that information later.

The rule of thumb with the resume and the interview is to demonstrate your skills. Whenever possible make the resume an example of what you can do.

Consider how Ann did this:

Ann grabbed the attention of the news service and won an immediate offer with her resume. She presented her work history as a news story and had it printed in the same typeface on long strips of the kind of paper used by the service. At first glance her resume looked like it had actually come over the "wire." She used language common in the newswire stories like "Take One, Take Two" preceding descriptions of her skills. "North Eastern Action" was followed by descriptions of jobs she held in stations in Northern New York and the descriptions themselves sounded like the newswire stories.

Ann's calling card was modeled on the FCC license required of all radio personnel on the air. She had worked in radio for over twenty years. The card was a miniature of the license down to the color and typeface with one notable exception: Instead of "Federal Communications Commission" her card said "Famous Creative Communicator." Needless to say, when her resume came across the desk of the decision-maker at the news service it immediately caught his eye and overshadowed all the others. The resume was a sample of Ann's creative abilities and demonstrated in its language and form that she had a good understanding of what the newswire did.

In like manner, Jackson is a graphic artist who presented his resume as an example of his graphic-art work.
He used spacing, bold lines, and graphic bullets to draw
attention to information he wanted transmitted. Just
looking at the resume showed the type of work Jackson
could produce.

Not all job histories are conducive to these creative
forms. Don't let that deter you. Throw down preconcep-
tions and limitations and see what you can come up with.
Even when you use a standard resume layout, the "func-
tional" resume is probably the best. Here the information is
divided into skills or functions you have performed rather
than a time-line of jobs. Sort your skills into categories
such as "supervision" or "coordination." Use these general
functions as the main topical headings and describe what
you can do rather than listing job after job and what you
have done.

THE JOB INTERVIEW

Think of a way to actually *show* the person who has the
power to hire you what you can do. You might bring
examples of your work to the interview. Artists, for example, always show a portfolio. Sidney kept a loose-leaf
notebook with information about himself where he kept all
his performance reviews. If something
appeared in the company newspaper
report on his projects, he added it.
And once in a while his name
appeared in the

community paper. "If your name appears in the paper, people assume you must be good. Of course, this is not really the case, but it makes a good impression," said Sidney. Bringing a sample of what you have done to the interview is persuasive and makes an impact.

Don't just tell—show and tell.

Prepare your presentation in advance. Convert tasks into skills. Show how the skills you acquired in the past can be used in this new context. Don't wait for the interviewer to make this connection. Always emphasize the service you have to offer. Words like "responsibility," "accomplishment," and "contribution" have more impact than "tasks" and "duties." Investigate the position and tailor your presentation so that you look like the perfect candidate.

Switching to a new line of work or a new career is a big change and not one to do glibly. Yet you should always hold it as a real possibility. Simply considering it can refuel your spirit.

You have options—you are not trapped and helpless.

In previous times, people often remained in one line of work until retirement. Things are different now. If you began work at age 25 and work until 65 (and we could question if one should "retire" at such a young age); that's 40 years—plenty of time for two, three, even four full careers. Mid-life career changes are common these days. It's a way to have a second start on life. Don't close your opinions and limit yourself. Look around and see what is possible.

We can find a way of life that is meaningful and purposeful, a way of life that makes your heart sing, a way of bliss.

—Hal Zina Bennett & Susan J. Sparrow
Follow Your Bliss

Chapter Ten

Think Powerfully

What you think—words and images flowing through your mind—exerts a tremendous influence on how you feel and act. Your ever-constant thinking becomes apparent when you try to quiet your mind. Try this now. *Simply quiet your mind for one minute.*

If you're like the rest of us, thoughts clamored into your mind from nowhere. Thoughts—your self-talk—fill your mind all the time, even when asleep. The mystics call this "the chatter." What you think about and how you think about it has a tremendous impact on how you feel about yourself, about your work, and how you act.

You can experience this right now. Bring to mind a somewhat unpleasant situation or encounter from the past. Imagine actually being in the situation and relive it for a few second, making it as vivid as possible. Continue to think about the unpleasant situation for several seconds as you notice what you experience.

Before reading on, take a couple of deep breaths and purposefully relax yourself. Put the memory of the unpleasant situation aside and recall your pleasant scene, making it vivid in your mind, while enjoying the warm nurturing feeling of relaxation.

What did you experience when recalling the unpleasant situation? How did you feel? Most people who do this experiment experience changes like quickening breath, increase in heart rate, tightness in the stomach, and other signs of activation because thinking about the unpleasant situation triggered the stress response.

Most people report that the sensations they experienced when thinking about the unpleasant situation are similar to those they experienced in the real situation. This is important because it illustrates the paradoxical nature of the human biocomputer. On the one hand, the mind is more complex than the most sophisticated computer ever developed. At the same time, the body is easily deceived. We respond to thoughts in the mind as if what we are thinking about is actually happening. That is, the body responds to thinking about the unpleasant situation in the same way as when actually experiencing it. You probably noticed the response in a mere thirty-to-sixty seconds.

You reside in a biocomputer. The words you think and the images you imagine are the programs that make the body run.

Thinking about unpleasant situations sends an instruction to the body to activate, much in the same way that a java script instructs your computer to run a particular routine. It is the thinking, and not the event that is the program or instruction. An unpleasant event occurs, you think certain things about that event, and those thoughts instruct your body to respond in a particular way. So while it seems that the event made you respond, it is actually the mental programs—which are simulations of reality—that make you respond. The biocomputer responds to thoughts about events and not the events themselves.

You can modify the programs that run your biocomputer.

The unique thing about your biocomputer is that *you* can modify your own programs. You may not be able to do anything about the event, but you can think about it in a variety of ways, each of which will instruct your body to respond in a particular way. What this means is that if you learn how to take command of your thinking, you can change your responses to stressful situations. You are not a helpless victim of circumstance—even though it may feel that way.

A DELICIOUS STRAWBERRY

A man traveling through a remote area encountered a hungry tiger, which chased him to a precipice where the man climbed down a vine hanging on the side of the cliff. Halfway down he noticed that below him were two more hungry tigers, looking up at him, licking their chops in anticipation. Then the man saw a mouse chewing at the vine upon which his destiny hung. Turning his attention to the cliff beside him the man saw a strawberry plant hanging out of a crag with one perfectly ripe, luscious strawberry growing on it. The man picked the berry, popped it into his mouth, and said, "Ah, delicious!"

FOCUSING

The man in the story focused his thoughts solely on the strawberry and its delicious taste, which instructed his body to experience pleasure. Because he did not think about the tigers, his body did not respond to their threat. Herein lies the secret to empowering yourself when you are confronted with unpleasant situations. You do not have to be a victim of the situation. By directing your attention and managing your thoughts, you can control how you feel and how you respond and thereby increase the quality of your moments to live your life more fully.

Words

Words are a vehicle for communicating information, but they also instruct your biocomputer to respond with particular emotional and physiological responses. This is the dynamic underlying the "pleasant scene". When you imagine the scene, the set of words and images you put into your biocomputer instructs your body to relax. Similarly, when you think—talk to yourself—about an unpleasant situation, words and images instruct you to stress your body. When you worry, anxious words in your mind keep you in a state of stress. Most people have poor thinking habits and indulge in negative, helpless self-talk that keeps them in a state of constant turmoil—distress. The following story about two monks illustrates how the constant chatter of words causes you to carry frustrations from work home with you.

TWO MONKS

Two monks were meditating as they walked along a muddy road. They came across a beautiful young woman trying to cross the road without soiling her shoes. Without saying a word, the first monk picked up the woman, carried her across the road and set her down.

Then the monks resumed walking without talking.
That evening when they reached their destination the
second monk said, "Why did you pick up that woman
this morning? You know women are dangerous." The
first monk replied, "I left her on the side of the road.
Are you still carrying her?"

The ease with which words trigger the stress response seems like a flaw in the human system. When you take a closer look, however, you'll see this is a survival mechanism. Survival is every organism's first priority. Below conscious awareness your basic operating system continually appraises information gathered through your senses. This appraisal involves a basic yes/no question: "Is there a threat?"

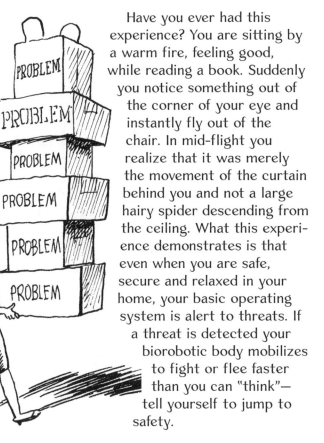

Have you ever had this experience? You are sitting by a warm fire, feeling good, while reading a book. Suddenly you notice something out of the corner of your eye and instantly fly out of the chair. In mid-flight you realize that it was merely the movement of the curtain behind you and not a large hairy spider descending from the ceiling. What this experience demonstrates is that even when you are safe, secure and relaxed in your home, your basic operating system is alert to threats. If a threat is detected your biorobotic body mobilizes to fight or flee faster than you can "think"— tell yourself to jump to safety.

USING HELPFUL THOUGHTS

If you study the actual words and sentences you tell yourself, you'll discover that most worrying and negative thinking makes you feel helpless. When you engage in a lot of helpless thinking you come to believe what you are saying to yourself, which increases your susceptibility to burnout. It becomes a vicious cycle because as people fall victim to burnout they tend to engage in more and more helpless thinking, which quickens the process. So it is vitally important to tune into your thinking and take corrective action if you hear yourself thinking in helpless ways.

When you keep telling yourself that you are helpless you become helpless

You can change the way you respond by changing the program—the words—in your mind. You accomplish this by substituting a helpful thought for the helpless one. For example, berating yourself for thinking, "Oh gawd, I blew it! I am an idiot!" is guaranteed to result in stress. In contrast, you will experience a greater sense of control—personal power—if instead you think, "I made a mistake, but I can learn from my mistakes." Both statements are "accurate" descriptions, but the first one is a helpless thought that generates feelings of loss of control, while the second way of thinking is powerful because it focuses on what you can do.

Suppose a project you're working on bombs miserably. Thinking "I've failed" is helpless thinking because it emphasizes your failure, whereas thinking, "It didn't work out" is more helpful because the failure is attributed to "it." Both thoughts are equally valid; the first registers as "threat" launching guilt and anxiety—powerful stressors, whereas the second prompts you to develop a plan of action. The first is a helpless thought; the second is a helpful thought.

Identify Helpful Thoughts

Helpless thinking is tenacious, becoming an entrenched habit difficult to dislodge. Fortunately, you can rework thinking habits and rewrite thought programs. It's a good idea to start off with just one area of helpless thinking rather than to attempt to change all your demoralizing thoughts simultaneously. For example, you may begin with helpless thoughts relating to George, someone you have difficulty dealing with. When you have some success changing thoughts related to George, you can take on another batch.

You must get down to the specific words to reprogram your responses.

You need to know exactly what you're thinking to reprogram effectively. The process is fairly simple. When you catch yourself thinking a helpless (negative, hostile, fearful, etc.) thought, jot the thought down, word-for-word. Continue doing this for a few days until you have a list of your frequent helpless thoughts.

Get a packet of ordinary 3 x 5 file cards. Transfer the helpless thoughts from your list onto the file cards, with one on each card. Leave the backs of the cards blank. When you feel relaxed and objective, take these cards one-by-one and rewrite each helpless thought into a helpful one on the back of the file card. Generally the helpful thought is a simple factual statement as illustrated in the table. You should end up with a packet of "flash cards," with a helpless thought on one side and a helpful one on the other

When Jackie wrote down her helpless thoughts she realized that she constantly said, "I'm sorry" and that doing so made her feel inadequate and lowered her self-esteem. She said, "It started out as a smart aleck remark from my boss, who said, 'I never apologize. It shows weakness!' So I started watching myself each time I said "I'm sorry" and damn if he wasn't right. Now I say, "Excuse me", "Pardon me", "Regretfully", or even "Oops" and I no longer get those feelings of inadequacy."

HELPLESS THOUGHTS	HELPFUL THOUGHTS
If I say 'no,' he'll be disappointed.	I can't meet everyone's expectations.
I have so much to do I'll have to work all weekend.	I can set priorities and work on important things first.
"It's an important session and I'm going to blow it."	"I can make a plan to control myself."
I made a big mistake!	I can learn from my mistakes without dwelling on them.
I was a fool to say anything.	I spoke up, that's what's important.
I'm a failure and going nowhere.	I am reliable and do a good job.
I've always been high-strung. I can' tchange.	That's just a bad habit. I can learn new and better responses.
I can't relax.	If I breathe deeply I'll relax a little.
I really blew it this time!	That's in the past. Next "time I can . . ."
My boss is a lousy supervisor! She never says what she really wants.	This is my chance to practice assertiveness and find out what she want.

Prompt Helpful Thoughts

Your helpful thought is unlikely to spontaneously occur; something must remind or prompt you to say the helpful thought to yourself. One way to do this is to find an activity you do frequently, such as going to the photocopy machine, answering phone calls, checking email, and getting a cup of coffee. Use the urge to engage in this frequent activity as a signal to remind you to read a helpful thought. For example, you might place your file cards next to the phone. Each time you need to make a phone call, use this as a signal to remind you to read and think the helpful thought on the top card. Making the call serves as a prompt to remind you to think the thought and a kind of reward for doing so. In this way helpful thoughts will be more available in your mind when you need them. The next step involves substituting a helpful thought for the helpless one in real situations.

THOUGHT STOPPING

When you notice yourself worrying, stop the helpless thought and substitute a helpful one. To do this you must know how to stop the thought. Try this experiment: Bring to mind a mildly unpleasant situation. Silently talk to yourself about the negative aspects of the situation. When you feel yourself getting worked up, yell "Stop!" inside your head to yourself. Notice what happens. Then switch your attention back to reading this book.

What happened right after you yelled, "Stop!"? Did your thoughts about the unpleasant situation stop—if only for a moment? This demonstrates the essence of thought stopping. It's a technique that is simple to do but takes practice to master. Usually after yelling "Stop!" the thought stops, but only momentarily.

Yelling, "Stop!" is commanding yourself to quiet your mind. As you have seen, this is practically impossible (without years of mediation training, anyway). The command empties the mind for a moment but it immediately fills back up with the most available thoughts—the worry.

Don't despair. The mind is paradoxical. While it has sophisticated computerlike capabilities, the mind can think only one thought at a time. This means if you quickly fill the void following "Stop!" with a helpful thought, you can crowd out the helpless one. This is the reason for writing down and practicing helpful thoughts. "Stop!" creates a break in worrying, but you don't have time to compose a helpful thought on the spot. Instead, have one ready and well-rehearsed because you'll have only a moment to make the substitution. Even then you'll probably discover that keeping your attention on the helpful thought will be difficult and you'll tend to drift back into helpless thinking.

THE MIND IS LIKE A WILD ELEPHANT

The mind is like a wild elephant that you must master. In mastering a wild elephant you begin by chaining it. But when first chained the elephant rears up on its hind legs, throws its trunk back, and roars. It flaps its ears, slaps its tail, and runs away.

If you are a good elephant trainer you don't scold the elephant, but simply grab the chain and pull it back. The elephant will try to run away again and again. When this happens you must pull it back. Again and again the elephant will rebel and again and again you must pull it back.

Eventually, the elephant will be tamed when it learns that you are its master. Then you will have great power because you can climb up on the elephant and ride it fast and far. When the elephant learns who is the master, it will no longer have to wear its chain.

Like any habit, persistent practice is required to dislodge the helpless thinking.

In the beginning you will probably find that your mind will rebel, like a wild elephant, and run back to helpless thoughts. Instead of criticizing yourself, just yell "Stop!" (silently—unless you're alone) and pull your mind back to the helpful thought. You may have to use thought stopping several times in a row, and pull your elephant mind back again and again—but with practice it will become easier and easier.

Direct Yourself

Following directions is helpful in the first stages of learning any complicated skill. When learning to ski, for example, it's helpful if your instructor observes and directs your attempts. She may call to you, "Now, shift your weight. Good, you've got it." You may have noticed that it helps to talk to yourself when you are learning a new skill. This is called self-directing.

Like learning tennis or skiing, learning to think in a new way is a complex skill, one made easier by following directions. *Talk to yourself.* Determine in advance what you are going to do and then direct yourself in a helpful way through the various performance steps. With thought stopping, for example, tell yourself to yell "Stop!"

Helpless thinking is as difficult to uproot as crabgrass.

Immediately after yelling "Stop!" tell yourself to think the helpful thought. Guide yourself through the thought and acknowledge yourself each time. Acknowledge noticing the negative thought and yelling, "Stop!" Acknowledge thinking a helpful thought even if you do slip back into helpless thinking. Notice what you have done well and point it out in a positive manner, as any good instructor would.

Practice on Your Mental Stage

Everything you do to fight helpless thinking is worth the effort. Go back to the data you collected and look for those situations that prompt helpless thinking. Select an easy to moderately difficult situation. For example, suppose seeing George prompts you to think, "I can't say 'No,' he'll be furious!" In preparing for your next encounter with George, know exactly what helpful thought you'll substitute. In your imagination, set the props for the encounter with George, and step onto your mental stage. *See* and *feel* yourself interacting with him. Hear the helpless thought in your mind. Direct yourself to yell "Stop!" Tell yourself to substitute the helpful thought. Tell yourself to notice feeling calm and in command. Tell yourself to acknowledge yourself for carrying out your plan. Talk yourself through each step. The more difficult the situation and the more entrenched the helpless thought, the more you should rehearse before a real life encounter.

WE LIVE IN A SIMULATION

An unending stream of images, sounds, and other data from the senses are synthesized, translated into words as simulations of events—although they feel "real". Of course no two events are precisely alike, but some are similar enough that we use the same words to describe them. In this translation process, similarities weigh heavier than differences. Because of this, something is lost, as raw data of the senses translates into words in your head. Our thoughts are simulations of the events and not the actual event. Rarely are these associations challenged. They become an automatic process. We respond to what we tell ourselves is out there—our simulations of reality—rather than to reality itself. We live in a simulation, mistaking the words and categories to which we have assigned the sensory data for the events themselves. This goes on rapidly without noticing.

Thoughts about an event become synonymous with the event itself.

You may think such things as "You made me angry!" or "He hurt me." But when you slow down the workings of your mind to closely observe what goes on you'll see that you respond to your interpretation of the event (appraisal) rather than the actual event itself. For example, "You said I was bad (event). That is a cruel and hurtful thing to do (appraisal). I'm hurt (response)." Stated another way, your mind gathers the data from its senses, converts it into words which yield a simulation of what's out there, then appraises it by asking "Is there a threat? Yes or no?" and then responds to the appraisal of the simulation, not the actual event.

We respond to our thoughts about the situation rather than to the situation itself.

Simulations Cloud Vision

Appraisals are based on past experience. An appraisal is a statement of what we expect. The more we encounter certain data, the less we pay attention to it. We give it brief notice, recognizing similarity to previous events, and then make a prediction. This is the appraisal. Then we respond to the appraisal—the simulation, the picture we've created within the biocomputer—and not to the actual event.

We may completely overlook valid but contradictory information. As a result of paying less attention to sensory data and relying heavily on expectations from the past, appraisals are ultimately based on selective perception because valuable information is blocked out. We simply don't see it because of what we expect to see, even though the information is there to be gathered.

An appraisal is a kind of stereotyping of experience.

We don't see the world as it is; we see what we think about the situation—a facsimile. This is a simulation. We can change what we "see" by changing our appraisal or judgement of the situation.

The Appraisal Process and Burnout

Without realizing it, we constantly monitor the events in our world. Our senses are always scanning the world and bringing in data that we subject to the appraisal: "Is there a threat?" When the answer is "yes" this threat activates the basic operating system and triggers the stress response.

The process does not stop here, however. There is a second appraisal: "Am I powerful? Do I have the power to stop the threat?" We respond based upon these two appraisals. The basic operating system flips into fight/flight in response to threat potential. Mood and behavior are a direct response to the appraisal of having personal power.

Expectations

At the heart of the appraisal is an expectation, an outcome prediction based on past experience. Expectations are easy to recognize by the "shoulds" and "shouldn'ts." "He should be able to set a clear goal." "She should be more reasonable." "He shouldn't talk to me that way." "The company should be fair."

The possibility of loss is implicit in any attachment.

Statements containing "should" or "shouldn't" are demands. They demand that the world conform to your expectations. Krishnamurti, a great Eastern philosopher, would say that you are attached to what you expect, clinging to a "should." He says that attachment leads to suffering. You suffer when you demand that the world conform to what you expect and refuse to accept what actually is.

When you engage in thinking based on expectations and "shoulds"—and we all do it—you are setting yourself up for suffering. Always implicit in an attachment is potential loss. If the expectation is not fulfilled—if your "shoulds" are not met—you suffer a loss. Even when things are going well, exactly as you desire, if you become attached and demand that it continue, then the threat of loss is present. Remember, a loss or a *potential* loss is always a threat. The stress response kicks in when faced with a threat.

LET GO OF ATTACHMENTS

"Should" thinking is the way most of us think. But it's not the only way to appraise events. You can change your reactions, including your emotions, by altering the way in which you talk to yourself about events. The key is to change your appraisals by reinterpreting the data.

Change the way you talk to yourself and you change the way you feel.

Any appraisal based upon an expectation or a "should" has the potential for causing a problem. You can get around this by substituting preferences for expectations. An unfulfilled preference is not a loss. It is something you'd like but don't demand. You are unattached. If the preference is actualized you win and have more of what you want in your life. Unfulfilled expectations, on the other hand, tend to be seen as catastrophes and personal affronts. We respond to them as threats, which activates the basic operating system, triggering the stress response.

Change expectations to preferences
Change "shoulds" to "wants"

Suppose, for example, a friend is late. If you say to yourself, "She is late again and she shouldn't make me wait!"
you will probably feel violated and angry. Instead you could
think, "She is late. I prefer that she be on time but she is
not because she is a poor time manager." In the first
instance, you "expect" the friend to be on time and tell
yourself that the lateness is a violation of social etiquette
and being disrespectful to you. Then you respond with hurt
and anger to being treated improperly. In the second
instance, you appraise the situation as not having a preference met rather than as an example of mistreatment. Here
you respond more directly to the event—the friend's lateness. Without the emotions interfering, you can concentrate on the best course of action.

IS THAT SO?

*A concerned brother demanded that his pregnant
sister tell him the father's name. "It was the Old Man
on the hill," she lied. Furious, the brother stomped up
the hill to the Old Man's house. "Look what you've
done to my sister you evil Old Man!" he yelled. "Is
that so?" the Old Man replied.*

*Time went by. After the birth the brother stomped
up the hill with the baby. "This baby is your doing.
You must take it!" "Is that so?" the Old Man replied.*

*The Old Man fed and cared for the baby. As it grew
he came to love the child who brought much joy into
his lonely life. But the girl grew remorseful and
confessed her lie to her brother.*

*Shamefaced the brother climbed the hill again. "Old
Man," he said, "I am sorry that I wrongly accused you.
Now I'm taking the baby back to its mother where it
belongs." And the Old Man replied, "Is that so?"*

IS THAT SO?

Most of us would probably respond differently from the man in the story if we were wrongly accused. We'd probably say things like, "No, I am wrongly accused. I shouldn't be wrongly accused and it is terrible that I am!" Chances are we'd respond by getting very upset. When the Old Man says, "Is that so?" he is neither agreeing with the brother's rendition of events nor is he saying that he likes the situation. Asking "Is that so? Are those the facts? Is that what she said?" doesn't tend to trigger an emotional response. Without the negative emotions, the Old Man suffers less and is more clearheaded. There is nothing to stop him from getting his lawyer to fight the situation.

The next time you are given bad news, try asking "Is that so?" instead of telling yourself, "This is terrible!" or "He shouldn't do that to me!" It's a powerful response. Try it.

USE POTENT LANGUAGE

Another way to change an appraisal is to use potent language, language that emphasizes personal power. This is tricky but with practice you can learn to do it. We're all familiar with the benefits of changing "the glass is half empty" into "the glass is half full." Both are "true" statements, while one is a loss-type of picture of the world, whereas the second is a more abundant picture.

Redefine the data coming into your senses in a way that makes you feel potent.

The essential key is to look for ways in which you can control the situation, ways in which you have a choice or can assume responsibility. If things don't turn out as you desire, for example, instead of saying to yourself, "This is a disaster and I'm helpless," it's more helpful to say to yourself, "This is a challenge and I will find a way to overcome it." Rather than "I'm ruined," think, "This is a new beginning, a rebirth."

The more difficult the situation, the more crucial the way you talk to yourself about it. For example, prisoners of war who survived often viewed the brutal guards they had to endure as their teachers.

When adversity is seen as an opportunity to learn you feel more in control.

"This is a lesson, a test. I am not helpless. *I can do* something—I can develop my skills to deal with this difficulty." Aleksandr I. Solzhenitsyn describes how he saw adversity as a teacher, which helped him survive years in one of the worst Russian prison camps:

HOW TO FACE DIFFICULTIES

"How to face difficulties?" he declared again. "In the realm of the unknown, difficulties must be viewed as a hidden treasure! Usually, the more difficult, the better. It's not as valuable if your difficulties stem from your own inner struggle. But when difficulties arise out of increasing objective resistance, that's marvelous!

"The most rewarding path of investigation is: 'the greatest external resistance in the presence of the least internal resistance.' Failures must be considered the cue for further application of effort and concentration of willpower. And if substantial efforts have already been made, the failures are all the more joyous. It means that our crowbar has struck the iron box containing the treasure. Overcoming increased difficulties is all the more valuable because in failure the growth of the person performing the task takes place in proportion to the difficulty encountered!"

—Aleksandr I. Solzhenitsyn
The First Circle

If this tactic can help prisoners endure twenty-five years of hard labor and demeaning treatment, it can help you handle problems in your work situation. You'll be surprised at how effective it is to change your picture of the problem and the way that you talk to yourself about it. Think back to the man on the vine looking at the straw-berry instead of the tigers. He did not succumb to helpless thinking; rather, he focused on what he could control—enjoying the strawberry.

Chapter Eleven

Develop Detached Concern

Burnout is a kind of job depression, a malaise of the spirit. It is not a matter of ability to perform—the victim is physically able to work, but interest is gone, enjoyment is empty, life is drudgery. Like a sophisticated computer unplugged, with the energy source turned off, the burnout victim is inoperable.

One difference between people who prevent burnout and those who succumb is that survivors find a third way. Burnout need not lead to failure or a destroyed, wasted life. It can be a catalyst to a new beginning. Those who accept the challenge find an opportunity to actualize a richer, fuller life.

Burnout can be a catalyst to a new beginning.

Like the man on the vine with the tigers above and below, the secret is to surrender. Stop demanding that the world be different from what it is. Instead, accept the situation and look inward. "What do I want? Who am I?" Within these questions lies a lifeline. Plug into an internal source of power and regain access to vast stores of ability and knowledge.

SEEK YOUR ENERGY SOURCE

THE WAY OUT OF BURNOUT

The third way, the way out of burnout can be found in exercising detached concern. This is often thought of a spiritual path, which many mistakenly think means leaving your profession, experimenting with drugs, dressing in baggy white or orange clothing, going to an ashram to find a guru, living a Spartan life, eating microbiotic foods, walking around with a blissful expression, and speaking in an esoteric, cosmic vocabulary. Such external changes mean nothing at all and do not bring about a spiritual experience. Detached concern has little to do with these sorts of things; it is something else entirely.

Be Like a Mirror

Detached concern is best discussed with metaphor. Imagine, for a moment, standing in front of a mirror. The mirror reflects your image, which is the nature of mirrors. When you move aside, the mirror stops reflecting you—it let's you go. The mirror doesn't whine, "Don't go. It's not fair that you leave. I'll keep reflecting you anyway." The mirror does not reflect the past or future but only what is in front of it at the moment. The mirror is detached and does not "cling" to images. This is not indifference or withdrawal; rather it is a total commitment to the activity at hand, reflecting an image in the now.

Mother Teresa

An example of detached concern is provided by Nobel prize winner, Mother Teresa of Calcutta. To the inquiry, "It must be dreadful working with these sick children and then so many die anyway. How can you stand their dying?" Mother Teresa is reputed to have answered, "We love them while they're here."

Like the mirror, she reflected a total commitment to what she was doing in the moment, namely nursing a sick child who may die in a matter of hours. She did not concern herself with worrying about the future or lamenting over a child who died yesterday.

WHAT IS DETACHED CONCERN?

Detached concern involves focusing all efforts into what you are doing at the moment, while remaining unattached to the outcome of your actions. Of course, you prefer that things turn out as you like, but you do not *demand* it. This does not reduce interest in what you are doing; rather this expression of personal power is characterized by more commitment. Energy is not wasted on regretting, doubting, or grieving for the past or worrying about the next moment.

Practice Good Sportsmanship

The idea of detached concern is difficult for most Westerners to grasp. One parallel in our world is sportsmanship. A good sport is expected to play hard to win (concern), but not to insist upon winning (detached). Athletes who stomp off the court, kick the lockers, and swear at opponents when they lose and are considered to be poor sports. It is more important to be a good sport than it is to win.

DON'T DEMAND THAT YOU WIN

Good sportsmanship and detached concern teach us that how you shoot the arrow is more important than hitting the target. Whether you are a chief executive or a newly hired clerk, a social worker or a paper pusher, immerse yourself in the moment, focus your attention on what you are doing, and let go of the outcome, good or bad. Events will not always be to your liking and you will not always win. Don't demand that you win. Instead, concentrate on playing a good game. Let losing teach you how to shoot the arrow next time. Don't cling to losing, either.

Like the monk walking along the muddy road, leave negative situations on the side of the road.

Detached concern is a state of being actively involved and committed to an action of the moment—yet unattached to the outcome. Interestingly enough, you'll find that acceptance of what is and focusing on the now brings calmness, greater ability to concentrate, and increased possibilities for deriving nurturing sustenance from your encounters with the world.

BE HERE NOW.

Be Yielding

Each day during the winter, snow fell on two trees—an oak and a pine—in a field. The firm limbs of the big oak tree supported the snow until the branches, no longer able to bear the weight, broke and fell. Next to the oak tree, the pine tree also accumulated snow, but its limbs were supple, not rigid. They bent to the ground and let the snow slide off, then returned to their original position. The pine survived the winter; the oak did not.

Flow around the rocks in life like water flowing downstream,

Be flexible. Don't be attached to a particular notion of the way things ought to be. Look for alternative and creative ways to reach your goals.

Shift Your Viewpoint

Philosopher Alan Watts once said, "Problems that remain persistently unsolvable should always be suspected as questions asked in the wrong way." Do you trap yourself into damned-if-you-do, damned-if-you-don't situations by the way you look at things?

Laugh a Lot

Practice finding humor in disaster. When you catch yourself taking things too seriously—think of the cosmic
chuckle and *laugh* the absurdity of it all. Satirize your
distress. Imagine yourself in a Charlie Chaplin script.
Pretend you are a stand-up comedian and that the disas-
trous situation is material for your next gig.

Laugh at your distress.
You'll save your sanity,
your health, and your perspective.

Leave It on the Side of the Road

Ceaseless worrying about office politics and impossible
aspects of your job consumes the vital moments of your
life. Through this internal chatter that we call worry, you
carry these stressors with you everywhere you go. Remember the story about the monk who carried the woman
across the muddy road and how the second monk upset
himself by worrying about it all day. As these psychological
toxins grow you become cut off from experiences themselves, unable to derive pleasure or substance from your
daily routine because you don't connect with the real world
at all.

As you saw in the quiet-mind experiment in the last
chapter, it is exceedingly difficult to turn off self-talk. The
key to quieting the chatter lies in the paradox of acceptance. Acceptance doesn't mean to be passive or a victim,
but to not make the situation a catastrophe, which triggers the stress response. By observing and accepting your
thoughts you can quiet the chatter. Self-observation is
most important. By watching your thoughts dispassionately
you eventually come to know yourself. Look. Accept. Don't
attempt to change. See who you are. This leads to self-
mastery, the eternal source of personal power.

APPRAISAL MODES

There are, many parts of yourself to look at and many ways of looking. The appraisal mode ladder provides a lens for looking at how you interpret sensory data. The most primitive appraisal occurs in the associative mode.

Associative Mode

When you think the word "black," what is the first association that comes to mind? Most people say "white." What do you associate with "boy"? "Girl" is probably the first association. These unchallenged associations form the basis of "automatic thinking", which is a kind of shorthand, with one or more words conveying the entire meaning about a situation. They are irratio-nal fleeting thoughts like "never appreciated," "she's so mean," "always losing," or "not fair." What burnout victims tell them-selves can be contrary to factual evidence as well as overgeneralized, absolutist, one-sided, and dogmatic.

This emotionally based self-talk *sounds like* the truth to you inside your mind, so it goes unchallenged and you accept things you say to yourself that you would never accept if someone else said them to you.

This is essentially what occurs during the associative ap-praisal process. Something simply comes to you, just pops into your mind. Associations can be so fast that you're not aware of them at all. There's no chance of self-control until you know your associations. Try the following simple "looking exercise" for seeing automatic associations.

The Multipetaled Flower

Relax with the method you prefer and imagine the center of a flower without petals. Place a word that represents the object of your study in the center of the flower. Focus on the word and notice what thoughts come to you. Note the association, whether you understand it or not. Make the association into a petal and tack it to the flower. Return your attention to the word in the center of the flower and repeat the process for several minutes.

Don't struggle to find an association; instead assume a passive stance and wait until something comes into your mind. Long-forgotten programmed associations will begin to surface. Simply observe each association and, like in the game of Pin the Tail on the Donkey, tack the petals of association onto the flower. Then bring your attention back to the word in the center of the flower. Don't be seduced into tangents by tantalizing associations.

A good word to start with is "work." Relax yourself and imagine the word "work" in the center of the flower. Notice what comes to you. Try this for about two minutes. Don't judge yourself by these associations or try to change them. Just look at them. You will learn a little more about yourself and your basic programming. Many find it helpful to jot down the associations discovered in a personal journal.

This exercise is helpful in exploring barriers. For example, you could place a word representing a troublesome decision, or the name of a person you have difficulty communicating with, in the center of the flower. Associations that come provide valuable insights and needed information for determining a course of action.

Fixed-View

Much as the name implies, fixed-view appraisals yield a single interpretation of a particular situation. The possibility of another interpretation is never considered. You actually believe your view *is* reality. A dangerous assumption! Fixed-viewers see rewriting the appraisals as lying. They assume there is one "correct" interpretation that cannot be improved upon.

People who think this way believe that the way they see the world is the one and only way; anyone who doesn't share their view is clearly wrong. Not only does this create the potential for conflict and breaks in communication, but the person is buffered from the real world and doesn't see the buffer. With each rigid judgement, you forfeit a little personal power.

When you believe your view is the only real one, you ignore the intervening interpretation and thereby lose a way to alter your responses. You have given over power to the knee-jerk reaction upon which the judgement is based. When your view is one of helplessness and frustration, feeling boxed in and caught in a double bind or an unfulfilling world, you are headed for burnout. This is a stumbling point for many burnout victims. By clinging to powerless appraisals they aid and abet their own burnout. Here is a story about fixed-view thinking:

A CUP OF TEA

A professor visited a Zen master who invited him to tea. The master poured the tea into the professor's cup. When the cup was full he continued pouring the tea until it overflowed onto the table.

Shocked, the professor exclaimed, "It's overflowing. It's full—no more will go in!"

"Like this cup," the master said, "you are full of your own opinions. How can I show you Zen unless you first empty your cup?"

Your ability to learn and to adapt is a source of personal power. Fixed-view appraisals make learning difficult, if not impossible. Assuming you already know what is going on and what it means, you do not look. Quality of learning is directly proportionate to the quality of feedback you receive from experience. By not looking at the incoming data, you are cut off from the feedback needed to learn. Consequently you continue clinging to a fixed-view even if it is no longer applicable. The fixed-view becomes a self-imposed trap.

Multiview Mode

Making the transition from the fixed-view to the multiview is rarely easy. The fixed-view is attractive because it gives the sense that everything fits very neatly into place. All challenges and contradictions have been carefully screened out or categorized. There is no contrast, no contradiction, nothing to remind you that this view of things is but one of many possibilities. You've got to break the habitual mind-sets that blind and prevent you from seeing the world. Multiview thinking brings power because it offers a choice. When you have a choice you're not helpless.

A handy tool for breaking mind-set is the **paradox**. Ambiguity and contradiction befuddle fixed thinking. Look at the sketch. What was the first thing you saw? You probably saw a rabbit. As you continue studying this sketch you'll see an ambiguity and then a duck emerging. Notice how your attentiveness and curiosity increased as

you looked at the picture. Perhaps there's even a third entity in the sketch. Philosophers have appreciated the transcendental qualities of the paradox for centuries.

Stories with a paradoxical twist are used to aid students of Zen and Sufism to see in a different way. And in fact, we in the West have also had a tradition of learning from stories. Think of the fairy tales you grew up with and the parables Jesus told. Try one for yourself. Consider the following Zen story.

THE SOUND OF ONE HAND

The student listened intently as the master clapped his hands and said, "This is the sound of two hands when clapped together. What is the sound of one hand clapping?

The student went to his room to consider the puzzle. During his contemplation he heard someone playing a flute. "Ah, I have it!" he thought. But when he played a flute for the master, he said, "No, no, that is the sound of a flute being played." As the student contemplated the question again, he heard some water dripping. "I have it now," he thought, and went to show the master. "That is the sound of dripping water, not the sound of one hand," said the master.

Again the student contemplated. He heard the sighing of the wind, but the master rejected that sound. Then he heard the cry of a bird, but the master rejected that sound as well. For almost a year he pondered what the sound might be. When the student at last let go he heard the soundless sound of one hand clapping.

It is contradictory to ask someone to demonstrate the sound of one hand clapping. Within the normal frame of reference one hand can't clap. So what can that sound be? In pondering such a paradox, you can break out of your fixed-view. Solving the riddle requires stepping outside your mind-set and looking at the question in a different way. The more you're able to do this, the more personal power you have, which enables you to be the master of your appraisals rather than a slave to them. Try this Sufi story.

A YOUNG MAN'S SEARCH

A young man was searching for knowledge which he thought he could find through experience. He wanted to know what was beyond the ordinary life. He went into the world, experienced many things, and went many places.

One day he arrived at a cave of an ancient sage who sat with a crystal in front of him. The young man was intrigued, as he gazed into the crystal. He was amazed by what he saw. There were things he'd never even heard of or even imagined possible. The young man asked the master, "I do not want to be a spectator. I must experience these wonders myself."

*"Step inside." the sage said as he invited the young man
to step into the crystal. Filled with wonder, the young
man found he could, indeed, walk into any of the scenes
he had seen in the crystal*

*After a short while the young man stepped out of the
crystal again. The sage handed him a hammer and the
young man smashed the crystal and walked away
without saying a word.*

The story entices and tickles the mind, encouraging
you to try on one interpretation after another. Within the
paradox lies a key for surviving the organization and
preventing job burnout. After an intensive study of the
distribution of burnout symptoms within the organization,
Abraham Zelnick and his group of Harvard Graduate Business School scientists drew this conclusion:

*"Bureaucratic practices set limits to the assertion of
power by individuals in the organization, but the possession of power in organizations reduces the harmful
consequences of bureaucracy to the individual. **Therefore survival in bureaucracies falls to those individuals who know how to negotiate a double-bind situation, while advancement in bureaucracies falls to
those individuals who can make an opportunity out
of a paradox."***

The man dangling on the vine above the hungry tigers
was in a damned-if-you-do, damned-if-you-don't situation.
By focusing his attention on the strawberry and altering his
appraisal of the situation, he was able to negotiate the
double bind and regain his power. Exercising your mind
with stories such as these develops the ability to make
opportunities out of paradoxes. At first it is simply a
mental exercise. But the stories act as a catalyst. As your
skill increases you'll be able to transfer what you've learned
to the frustrating ambiguities and contradictions at work.
You'll be able to use multiview thinking, rather than being
stuck in the fixed-view mode that the organization promotes. But these skills and abilities do not come instanta-
neously. They require much practice and contemplation.

Look For A Third Way

We think in dichotomies. The moment is pleasurable or painful. When it's painful we want to fight it or flee from it. Too often these two options are of little help. By developing your ability to make multiviewed appraisals you can find a third way: not fighting, not fleeing, but the way of acceptance, surrender. Surrender is not typically equated with mastery or power, yet surrender can be a powerful response.

Consider the sailboat. The boat skims along the top of the water not by fighting but by surrendering and going with the wind. A third-way appraisal helps in any difficult, unpleasant situation. Think of the frustration as your teacher. If your boss, for example, is vague and ambiguous when telling you what to do, accept this person as he is. He is your teacher and this is an opportunity to learn to work in a vague and ambiguous situation. When you pass this lesson your boss will no longer be a problem for you, nor will vagueness and ambiguity.

DETACHED CONCERN

Detached concern is a mode of nonappraisal. The thinking mind is silent. Without your meddling thoughts you respond directly to your senses. There are no criticisms; no congratulations, no judgment, no warning, no thinking at all. There is awareness only. Without thoughts to continually drag you into the past or the future, you can be truly in the moment.

Tim Gallwey, the Inner Game specialist, refers to this state as being "out of your mind." This does not mean out of control, however. In fact, when operating in this mode your abilities are synchronized and fine-tuned, and you function at your best.

SKIING OUT OF YOUR MIND

. . . your busy, chattering mind stops altogether and you enter into a world that is pure experience. You are calm, quiet, immersed in your activity. There is no separation between action and awareness, thinking and doing. You are in total harmony with yourself and your surroundings, and all else—time, space, past, and future—pales before the present moment. . . . "The usual mental struggle—trying to do everything right, worrying about how we look or about falling and failing—is forgotten. Enjoyment is so intense that we don't even think of making a mistake—and we don't. The thinking mind is in a state of rest; awareness is at a peak. For a time, self-imposed limitations are forgotten; we are skiing unconsciously."

—Tim Gallwey
Inner Skiing

Performing while "out of your mind" is what Gallwey calls the "breakthrough mode" because when you get out of your mind you make physical, creative, and spiritual breakthroughs. Without the diversion of your internal conversations and inquisitions you can tune in completely. There is no barrier between you and the world. Whether you are skiing, delivering a speech, working at a drafting table, or raking the lawn, when you're "out of your mind" you feel plugged in and energized. You and the task merge into one. You perform at your peak and the experience refuels you. You're not in a state of nothingness simply because the thoughts have ceased. Thinking has been replaced by awareness. You are alive and aware of being alive. What you are doing is less important than that you are doing.

Detached concern is a higher level of consciousness that can take a lifetime to evolve. Some call it the "master game" and believe it to be the only game in life worth playing. It doesn't matter if you are a housewife, a civil engineer, an artist, or a politician. What you do is only the canvas on which you paint that beautiful picture. Learning to achieve this sublime state of being, this continual state of being turned-on is the path with a heart. It feeds and nurtures you.

What you do is unimportant.
It's *how* you go about doing it that counts.

Directions can be stated in two deceptively simple words: *Just look.* Awareness is the higher self. Thinking interferes with awareness. By throwing up a smoke screen of speculations and interpretations, awareness is dimmed. Awareness is infinitely superior to thinking, but letting go of thinking is scary. We believe that without the thinker—the self that continually talks to you—we will be helplessly out of control. But reviewing those moments of peak functioning—the breakthroughs—you'll notice that you were out of your mind and not thinking. In other words, with your thinker turned off you performed without analyzing. Who was in command when you were out of your mind? This is the question that muses the sages. The self that was in command is your higher self. Many people do not realize this self exists. The language of this self is awareness, not words. Try the following simple awareness exercise.

WHO IS THERE?

Close our eyes and notice your sensations. Feel the surface beneath you. Notice your clothes touching your skin. Notice the sounds around you. Don't dwell on their meaning, just notice how they sound. Notice these sensations and let them be.   Notice your feelings. What is your mood? Do nothing about these feelings. Simply be aware of them and let them be. Notice your thoughts. What are you thinking about? Notice the tone. Don't change the thoughts, just be aware of them. How does it feel to be you right now? Notice who is noticing.

The alert feeling this exercise induces is awareness. By simply observing, you tune in. Achieving higher consciousness cannot be done by force. The mind will rebel, you will have a mutiny. Most people have given their thinker far too much power. The only way to control the mind is to tune into it and tame it. Become aware of your basic operating system, of your movements, of your feelings, of your thoughts.

It is through observation that you can tame your selves to become your own master.

To reach higher consciousness you must understand that there is a you beyond your thinker. Consciousness evolves through a series of developmental steps. For example, the child in the womb is literally one with its mother. They separate at birth, but this separation is not immediately obvious to the child. One of the first steps in developing consciousness is the concept of "I" or ego. The child becomes aware that it is separate from the mother and from the world. It is a separate being. There is self and not-self.

Virtually everyone makes it through the first step of separating one self from the world, but far fewer attain the awareness of the self beyond thinking, feeling, moving, and sensing.

HIGHER AND LOWER SELVES

You have four lower selves. There is the instinctual self—the basic operator who maintains heartbeat, respiration, and other vital functions. There is the moving self, who takes care of getting you where you want to go. There's the feeling self, who tells you what you want. And there's the thinking self, who analyzes, interprets, decides, and directs. When allowed to take command, the higher self orchestrates the actions of the four lower selves. There are many exercises you can use to stretch and strengthen your abilities and guide you in connecting with your higher self. Interestingly, they all have one central activity: looking.

Watch Your Instinctual Self

By simply watching heartbeat, skin temperature, breathing, or muscle tension, you can gain control over these vital functions. In biofeedback, you notice particular sensations, like temperature in your hand, and associate that with the feedback sound. In the muscle-tensing exercise, for example, you observe tension and relaxation and compare these two sensations. Mastery over tension is achieved by watching, not controlling or trying to control.

Similarly, you can learn to slow the rhythm of your breathing by focusing your awareness on your breath. Exhale very slowly. Then inhale gently. Hold the breath momentarily and slowly breathe out again. Use a slow regular quiet effort. Don't strain. Imagine slowing your breathing rhythm down to the point where if a feather were held before your nose it wouldn't move. Simply be aware of your breathing.

Watch Tension While You Act

While walking in a steady pace, slowly count to ten while gradually tensing your body all over. Constrict the muscles in your calves and thighs, clench the hands and feet, and grit the teeth. At the count of ten you should be as tense as you can possibly be and still be able to move. Now while slowly releasing the tension count backward from ten to one. Let your body go limp. You should be at the count of one when your body is at its most relaxed point but still moving. Increase tension a notch or two until you feel just right. This is your optimal level for performance. You're not so loose that you can't function, but not so tight that movement is restricted.

Watch Your Feeling Self

The feeling self is the most difficult to study because it overlaps and interacts with the other selves. The feeling self is the great motivator, and only with motivation will you have the power to achieve anything real. With emotional involvement words are transformed into deeds, theory into action. The "theater of selves" provides an ideal arena for watching emotions.

The Theater of Selves

While remaining completely relaxed project your self onto your mental stage and imagine reenacting an encounter or event. Make no changes; do not criticize or evaluate. Dispassionately watch the self acting. How does he or she feel? Just notice the emotion with a nonjudgmental, observant attitude.

As you perfect this exercise, carry it into the theater of your daily life. If you must evaluate, limit it to simple ratings of the feeling. When observing anger, for example, let ten represent the most angry you can imagine feeling and let one represent the complete absence of anger. As you observe angry feelings, rate them from one to ten. Don't try to change the feeling; just become aware of it. Strive as far as possible to separate the sense of "I" from the physical sensations being studied.

When you become somewhat skilled in watching yourself "act" in the theatre of selves you'll make a curious discovery. By observing and at the same time not identifying   with the sensations, they will change little by little without your directly trying to change them.

Watch Your Thinking Self

Use the multipetaled flower exercise described earlier to watch associations. When you become proficient at that exercise, move to the "Who am I?" exercise. This involves a series of structured questions and answers. Begin with the question "Who am I?" Note what answer comes and then challenge the answer. After each challenge ask another question.

WHO AM I?

Question: "Who am I?"

Answer: "I am John." Challenge: "No, John is a
            name I call myself."

Question: "Who is the I called John?"

Answer: "I am an engineer." Challenge: "No,
            engineering is the work I do."

Question: "Who is the I who works as an engineer?"

Answer: "I am tired." Challenge: "No, tiredness
            is a feeling I experience."

Question: "Who is the I who feels tired?"

"Who am I?" is a rigorous exercise. At times no answer
may come. Notice and accept the silence. With practice
you will eventually discover the I who is the "higher self."
As a variation try the "Who am I?" exercise while observing
yourself reenacting an encounter on your mental stage.
After noticing how you feel, ask, "Who is the I who feels
angry (sad, happy, alone, etc.)?"

Watch yourself during your daily routine. Observe what
you are doing, feeling, sensing, or thinking. In a detached,
impartial, impersonal manner, ask, "Who is doing this?
Who is feeling this? Who is sensing these things? Who is
thinking these thoughts?" Wait and see what answers come
to you. Through this process you will see your mechanical
responses to external stimuli. One result of these practices
is that your attitude toward people, things, and events will
tend to gradually change.

Watch Your Acting Self

By practicing "intentional" doing you can generalize detached concern into your daily life and capture the magic
of the moment. Intentional doing is doing one activity with
complete attention. The activity can be anything you
choose.

In walking, just walk; in sitting, just sit;
and above all don't wobble.

—Saying of Yun-men

Determine what you are going to do and why. Set
definite limits—how long, to what degree, to what quality.
Clearly visualize the process before beginning. Picture the
tools, material, the forces involved. Begin doing the activity
you choose to practice with and just notice yourself doing
it. If you become distracted, stop all activity. Return to the
starting point, redefine the intention, and start over again.
Strive to keep an inner silence and practice simple awareness of what you are doing so that you can receive impres-
sions simply and directly, bypassing thoughts.

TIE YOUR SHOE LACES IMPECCABLY

One day Carlos and Don Juan were walking through a
steep ravine. As Don Juan paused to tie his shoe, a huge
boulder broke loose from the rock wall and came crash-
ing down to the floor of the canyon, landing just about
where the two would have been had they not paused.
Carlos gasped, "Had we not stopped, the boulder would
most certainly have crushed us to death!"

"Suppose," speculated Don Juan, "on some other day, in
some other ravine, I stopped to tie my shoe lace just as
another boulder broke loose precisely above us. That
time had we continued walking we would have saved
ourselves."

Perplexed, Carlos asked, "What can one do?"

"My only possible freedom is found in tying my shoe
laces impeccably," replied Don Juan. In other words, the
only solution to the dilemma of fate is to perform every
act consciously, impeccably.

—Don Juan
The Second Ring of Power

Use Teaching Stories

Teaching stories can help you look at your modes of thinking. The moral of the story is unimportant. This is not a "religious" experience. What is important is looking at how your mind works and at what comes into your mind. These associations reveal your programming. Follow the directions for the multipetaled flower but substitute a teaching story for the flower.

There are lots of teaching stories available, so don't restrict yourself to Zen stories. Fairy tales are fun to use and evoke interesting associations. Psychologist Eric Berne, founder of Transactional Analysis, believed that your favorite fairy tale is a mirror of your life's "script." For example, if *The Ugly Duckling* is a favorite, you might enact it in your imagination, and notice what associations come into your mind. There are lots of teaching stories to choose from: Bible stories, Greek myths, and ethnic tales are a few.

CONNECT WITH YOUR HIGHER SELF

Simple awareness or "just looking" plugs you into your "higher self"! The body changes shape and size, and the mind changes outlook, but the I of consciousness persists from birth to death unchanged. To know oneself is to find that point of consciousness from which observations of these changing moods takes place.

Thinking is a power that may bind you or set you free. But one result of just looking is that eventually you'll be able to get out of your personal self. Awareness makes all experience fresh. As you perfect these skills, you will know where you are going, what you are doing, and why you are doing it. The secret lies in remaining unattached to the results of your activities and measuring success and failure in terms of inner awareness rather than outward achievement.

Build a Mental Retreat

A moment of mental quiet is often looked upon as a moment wasted. We persuade ourselves that we do not have a half hour to spend sitting quietly. However, energy invested in seeking will come back to you tenfold. With your increasing power you will be able to calm yourself in difficult situations, focus attention into intense concentration, rally abilities to perform at your peak, and pull from within new, creative

The mental retreat is a personal place constructed to your own specifications. It is your place, made for you, where you can regroup and refuel. The mental retreat provides an unending power source available any time, any place. In building the retreat, most important is that it works for you. Modify the guidelines presented here to meet your unique needs.

The retreat is helpful because it is one that is easy to be in any time, any place. You do not have to be passive or go to a secluded place to use the retreat. You can be active. Project the retreat around you so that what you are doing is in the center of the retreat. As you are doing something—leading a board meeting, driving on the freeway, writing a report—look at what you are doing. Notice your lower selves: what you feel, what you think, how you move, what you sense. Remember to only watch and not to judge, criticize, or even compliment. The more you do this, the more benefits you will reap.

By watching yourself while "doing" you can find contentment in any situation. Even in the worst conditions you'll find a path through the shadow of death. The more you use your mental retreat in this way, the more your ability to concentrate on what you are doing will increase. So, you can expect the quality of your work to improve. And finally, you will be living each moment fully. But these are not things you can whip out a credit card and buy. You must work for them. It is a lifelong process.

Guidelines

When you wake up in the morning, your first responsibility is to confront your Self. Yet, most people neglect doing this in favor of ruminating over the latest hassle. We tend to give activities and problems priority rather than tuning into the energy source, which can fuel activities and solve problems. Visiting your mental retreat is a helpful habit. Make it a normal part of your daily life. The best results are achieved by daily practice. Don't demand grandiose commitments of yourself. Start out small and develop a habit that you can expand on. Once you learn how to use it, you can enter your mental retreat any time, any place because you carry it with you.

In the beginning it is easiest to visit your retreat when you're comfortable. An easy body posture helps to put the mind at ease. It's best if you sit up rather than recline on your back. Choose a time when you will not be disturbed and when digestion is at rest. When learning to use the retreat use the same quiet spot or room every day if possible. Select a comfortable spot to sit. Develop a habit in small steps. You might begin with only ten minutes. Don't rush into it. When this feels natural, extend the time gradually to a half hour or more. Morning is a good time because it sets the tone for the day. Early evening is also a good time because it helps you to unwind from the day and provides a pleasant transition into evening. Just before sleeping is a good time, too, because it helps you relax and prepare for a restful sleep.

The first visits to the mental retreat are the hardest.

You will be bombarded with intruding thoughts and dis-carded memories. Expect this. Irrelevant thoughts will drift into your head. As soon as you become aware of the distraction, notice it, dismiss it, and begin at the point where you left off. It is difficult to concentrate for fifteen minutes or more. Persist. The side benefits of using your mental retreat include the development of intellectual discipline and the power of concentration that you can carry into all facets of your work.

Struggle is part of the dance of life.

Visiting your mental retreat will energize you, but it won't remove struggle from your life. Struggle provides resistance against which you exercise your selves, both higher and lower. And as you develop your abilities, the struggles will only become more difficult because the magnitude of the struggle is proportionate to the extent of your abilities. Interspersed among the struggles is joy. Even in the dreariest of situations, there's always a crag in the cliff where a strawberry grows. You must look to see it. Let expectations and attachments go. Accept the joys of the moment. For even struggle is doing and when you're aware, there's always joy in doing. When you can kiss this joy you will have the key to preventing burnout.

KISS THE JOY AS IT FLIES

He who takes to himself a joy
Doth the winged life destroy,
But he who kisses the joy as it flies
Lives in eternity's sunrise.

—William Blake

Chapter Thirteen

What Managers Can Do to Prevent Burnout

Absenteeism, on-the-job accidents, drug and alcohol use, conflict, substandard performance, and other signs of worker malaise are everywhere. A World Labor Report of the United Nation's International Labor Organization estimated that stress-related diseases such as ulcers, high blood pressure, and heart attacks cost the U.S. economy more than $200 billion a year in absenteeism, compensation claims, and medical expenses. The problem is not restricted to the United States. The report called job stress a "global phenomenon." For example, in a French survey, 64 percent of nurses and 61 percent of teachers complained of stressful working conditions. Stress claims by government employees in Australia increased 90 percent in three years in the 1990s. The UN agency report claimed job stress is a worldwide plague that afflicts British miners and Swedish waitresses just as it burns out Japanese schoolteachers and American executives.

While everyone is not a manager in an official sense, we all manage other people. We manage our coworkers, partners, spouses, children, and friends. We can do this in a way that encourages cooperation, or in ways that undermine it. At the same time, our coworkers, partners, spouses, children, and friends manage us. So we should all be concerned with interacting with others in such a way as to encourage enthusiasm and feelings of empowerment.

Job burnout is a motivational problem that can occur in any situation in which people feel they cannot win and feel helpless to change it. Traditional methods of leading and motivating people no longer seem to be working. The results of the UN study pointed to lack of control as a key factor in the high stress levels they observed. Skills lie dormant while interest in working wanes. Work becomes a chore.

IS YOUR STAFF BURNING OUT?

Instructions: Using a scale from 1 to 10, with 1 being "not at all descriptive" and 10 being "very descriptive," rate how descriptive each of the following statements is of your staff.

_____ 1. Employee turnover is high.

_____ 2. People are just putting in time.

_____ 3. Substance problems interfere with performance.

_____ 4. The absenteeism rate is high.

_____ 5. There is a lot of conflict.

_____ 6. Directives are not followed.

_____ 7. There is sabotage.

_____ 8. People cheat and steal.

_____ 9. Deadlines are not met.

_____ 10. There is a high rate of rework.

_____ 11. Back stabbing is commonplace.

_____ 12. Office politics interferes with performance.

_____ 13. Productivity is low.

_____ 14. People are confused about goals.

_____ 15. There is a sense of hopelessness.

_____ 16. There is little esprit de corps.

___ 17. People are secretive.

___ 18. People don't socialize much off the job.

___ 19. Teamwork is poor.

___ 20. Layoffs are common.

___ 21. There is a lot of complaining.

___ 22. There is not much participation.

___ 23. People are just out for themselves.

___ 24. People have little input into management decisions.

___ 25. Threats seem to be the best motivator.

SCORING:

25 - 75	Comfort Level: Your staff is exhibiting a few signs of burnout.
76 - 145	Caution Level: Your staff is exhibiting a moderate degree of burnout. Preventative action is advised.
146 - 200	Chronic Level: Your staff is exhibiting numerous signs of burnout. Ongoing corrective action is essential.
201 - 250	Crisis Level: Your staff is exhibiting full-blown burnout. Immediate crisis intervention is required to prevent organizational breakdown.

FOUR TOOLS THAT EMPOWER

Empowered employees have a feeling of "I can do and I can succeed by doing." Employees who feel they can impact on their work and can "win" by doing a good job retain their enthusiasm and are more motivated. They are also an asset to the company. The challenge to management is to orchestrate the work of employees, to draw upon and develop employee talents to focus their energy and efforts, and to coordinate the interaction of numerous employees and the flow of their output.

Empowered employees—employees who have a sense of control over their job tasks—are resistant to burnout.

There are four ways in which managers can increase the feeling of controllability among their staff: goal setting, feedback, reinforcement, and participation. Each encourages a feeling of mastery at work. Used in unison they are the most promising way to prevent burnout and they have a positive impact on productivity.

Goals

Goals are important because they provide a target. Without a goal the worker is like a ship without a destination, going around and around, never making progress.

A goal provides direction— something to shoot at.

Goal setting has a highly beneficial impact upon performance when combined with quality supervision and feedback. The goal provides something to aim for and challenges people to stay focused and interested. Goals help people develop, firm up, and stretch their skill muscles. Who sets the goals and how they're set impacts on productivity. When employees participate in goal setting they typically set higher goals and reach them more often than do those who are assigned a goal.

The nature of the goals is also important. Vague goals such as "do your best" or "give it your best shot" are really no goal at all and can be frustrating. Industrial research indicates that when goal setting is combined with quality supervision, production goes up; when goals are combined with poor supervision or no supervision at all, frustration and turnover is the result. In other words, goals alone are not enough.

Participation

The more influence people have over decisions directly related to their work, the better. All things considered, the average worker in this modern day is still

treated as being not much more reliable or trustworthy than a child. While workers are adults who make important decisions about their lives and carry them out, as soon as they enter the workplace, opportunities for independent judgment are withheld. Someone else makes them. Workers are seldom treated as responsible self-managing adults.

Participation helps make employees "burnout-resistant."

Numerous studies indicate that when given an opportunity to participate in goal setting, for example, employees set more rigorous goals and reach them more often than when they did not participate. Companies have much to gain by increasing the participation of their workforce. Participation opens communication channels. Workers know more about their jobs and impediments to performance than anyone else. Participation provides management with access to this vital information. Chances are employees will work harder, and the company will benefit by tapping into this reservoir of knowledge and skills. Participation, in theory, has been promoted for years; the difficulty is in implementing it.

Feedback

For goals to be effective in increasing motivation, a catalyst—feedback—must be present. The worker who receives no feedback on performance is much like a blindfolded archery student. Without seeing where the arrow hits, the archery apprentice has little chance of becoming a master. Feedback is vital to learning. Without feedback, goals are useless. Feedback is the yardstick we use to measure performance.

Feedback tells workers how close they've come to the bull's eye.

Based on feedback the next effort can be fine-tuned. Working without feedback is much like the athlete in training for the hundred-yard dash without a stopwatch. How can one evaluate the run, tell if there's been improvement, or determine what adjustments in performance to make? Feedback facilitates learning, and giving feedback is the cornerstone of quality supervision.

Acknowledgment

When and how you pay attention to employees is important. Often, managers forget about the power of personal attention, the most universally potent motivator. The effective manager is alert for and acknowledges small improvements. Acknowledgement that comes days or weeks after quality performance has little motivational clout. This is why Christmas bonuses, for example, tend to fail to influence motivation. They arrive too late. The sooner the reinforcement is administered the greater its impact on future performance.

Attention is the most potent motivator.

TASC PLUS
FOR QUALITY MANAGEMENT

Poor supervision is probably the single largest source of burnout. No one is surprised to hear that the problem is worst with authoritarian managers who forbid any exercise of personal power whatsoever. But few realize that the manager at the other extreme—the good guy—can have an equally demoralizing effect. Equating being liked with good supervision can be a disaster. Unfortunately, most companies make the erroneous assumption that good supervision comes naturally. It does not. Being a good manager requires skills as complex as those of a good psycho-therapist or a good defense attorney, for example. Each requires precision-tuned people skills. Managers need to know how to establish clear job standards, set specific output goals, give helpful feedback, notice and acknowledge on-task behavior, and troubleshoot performance problems before they become crises, in addition to decision-making, planning, coaching and leading skills.

Most managers are aware that implementing basic manage-ment tactics will have a dramatic impact on staff satisfaction and motivation. The problem is how to do so.

THE BEST MANAGERS ARE
THOSE WHO FUNCTION AS COACHES.

Coaching bosses don't just assign tasks and oversee work; they teach people to be good performers. The best managers develop the potential within their people, creating an invalu-able product for the company—a trained, motivated workforce. Few of us have ever had formal training in how to work. The public school system teaches how to follow orders, to walk in line, and remember facts, but not how to work, which includes determining priorities, setting goals, maintaining high motivation, and intentionally doing tasks.

When managers act as trainers (and at higher levels, when executives act as mentors) there's a hidden benefit for the company. The workforce is constantly upgraded as people are brought up through the ranks. Quality supervision develops the human resources within the company rather than squandering them.

MANAGING PEOPLE'S WORK REQUIRES SOPHISTICATED SKILLS.

Unfortunately, training in management skills, especially for lower level managers, is often scarce. I have developed some basic principles in managing people at work that I refer to as "TASC Plus." TASC Plus is an acronym that stands for a simple but effective managing process that incorporates four essential ingredients for quality performance: goals, feedback, participation, and acknowledgement. TASC Plus is easy to remember and easy to use.

TASC Plus is a technique that incorporates all the features necessary to sustain high motivation and productivity among performers. TASC Plus is a prescription that guides managers in communicating expectations and acknowledging on-TASC performance. Each letter in TASC Plus stands for one of the steps.

TASC Plus		
T	=	Tell expectation & how performance compares.
A	=	Ask for suggestions
S	=	Set objectives.
C	=	Check data.
+	=	Acknowledge on-TASC performance.

TELL

T stands for Tell. Tell the performer your expectation, which is usually meeting a particular standard, and how his or her performance compares to it. **A standard is the performance goal or target that describes the specific output that the worker is responsible for producing. If no standard has been set then developing one is of primary importance.** When feasible the employee should participate in the setting of the standard.

Performance Standards

A standard of performance is an invaluable tool for managers, providing a method for identifying and measuring on-TASC performance. Based upon this information, the manager knows what to acknowledge. Without standards most managers fall into the trap of looking at factors unrelated to output. For example, whether or not a design engineer comes in promptly at 8 A.M. or is chronically 15 - 20 minutes late probably has little to do with the quality of his or her design. In contrast, chronic lateness would have a definite negative impact on the performance of an on-the-air news broadcaster.

A good standard allows a manager to differentiate among people so that he or she can provide them with fair individual treatment. One person may be performing above the standard and deserve acknowledgement; another may be below the standard but making steady progress toward it and should receive acknowledgement for that progress; yet another's performance may be dropping and trouble-shooting action is needed to turn it around. Good standards make managers' decisions easier, provide a basis for individual treatment, and encourage performance rather than conformity. Unfortunately, most managers haven't set standards for the jobs they oversee.

There are a number of sources of information helpful in setting standards. You can consult the company's official job standards as a first step, but don't rely solely on these. Aside from frequently being out of date, by necessity they must be general enough to describe a job in a number of settings. Suppose, for example, "Office Assistant I" is an entry-level clerical position in any department. The job of Office Assistant I in the shipping department is likely to be very different from one in billing. It is difficult for company job standards to reflect these differences.

Another source of information is the relationship between jobs. What do others need from this person to perform their own function? The answer to this question reveals the essential output of the job. With technical and professional jobs the standard is often negotiated between manager and performer.

CHARACTERISTICS OF A GOOD STANDARD

The job standard is a description of the individual's output, which is a part of a long and complex chain of outputs that ultimately leads to accomplishing the overall organizational goals that usually involve making a profit by supplying a product or service.

Describe Output

The standard should describe an output. It is not a description of the behaviors or actions required to meet the standard but a statement of what result is expected. The output might be in terms of quantity, such as the number of machines inspected, number of vouchers processed, or number of complaints per quarter; of quality, such as the number of designs accepted or number of reworks; of time, such as the turnaround time, percent on-time, or response time; or of cost, such as the cost of downtime or cost per call. Standards that encompass more than one performance indicator such as specifying quality and quantity both are more effective than those relying on only one.

Specific

Good job standards are also specific. Vague standards lay the foundation for miscommunication and discontent. "Be prompt in answering the phone" is a vague standard. What is prompt? Does that mean to answer on the first ring? The third ring? Or within thirty seconds? The word "prompt" is open to interpretation. A better standard would be: "Answer the phone within three rings."

Achievable

The standard must be realistic. It must be something the person can actually achieve. It's best to provide a range. Reaching the low end gives the performer a feeling of success while reaching the high end provides a challenge.

Observable

The standard should be observable. At any particular time the manager as well as the performer should be able to answer "yes" or "no" to the question: "Has the standard been met?" A standard that is clearly stated in terms of observable output makes accountability (A-Count-Ability) possible.

Measurable

Finally, movement toward the standard should be easily measured. The more effort required to record an output, the less likely any data will be collected. And without counting it is difficult to determine whether or not the standard has been met.

Developing a standard is a difficult and challenging task. The difficulty lies in the area of measurement. It's pretty easy, for example, to evaluate the performance of a typist. You can look at the speed of typing, the layout of the work, or the number of errors. These variables are all easy to identify and easy to measure or count. Therefore, they make A-Count-Ability simple.

But what of jobs such as manager, public relations officer, or movie producer? What is the identifiable output for these jobs, and what are the observable behaviors that lead to the production of that output? Answering these questions is much more difficult but that does not mean it's impossible. When these questions aren't answered, how can people who perform these jobs tell whether or not they are performing well? And how is the manager to evaluate their performance?

TELL

When the standard has been determined and agreed upon, tell the individual how his or her performance compares to that standard. This feedback should be given in a simple, straightforward manner, using objective terms and avoiding judgmental, emotional, and vague words. Conciseness is important. Be clear and brief. Don't ramble, repeat, or go off on tangents that can come across as a harangue.

Use Quantitative Words

Whenever possible, use quantitative words: "Last week you were late two times" is better than "You've been late a lot." Don't defend the standard or apologize for it. Just state the expectation. Finally, deal with one standard at a time. Stringing three or four standards together will only overwhelm the person and not accomplish anything.

For example, to a floor manager you can say,

"Joe, one of your important functions is to motivate those you manage to peak performance. You can do this by making sure each of your people clearly understands his expected output and by checking each person's progress at least once a day. While checking the workers' charts you can let them know that you what they're doing to meet output goals (standard). I've noticed that you check everyone each day and are readily available to answer questions and that you take time to make sure that they understand the answer. But I rarely hear you commenting on good work (comparison)."

How you would respond to the following:

Bob, I've got to talk to you about the mail. You've got to be more efficient. I've been getting a lot of complaints about you. There have been just too many delays. People want their mail on time. Got that? And another thing. The place is a dump. Why don't you ever straighten things up around here?

This is a poorly stated Tell to say the least. It is bound to lead to miscommunication, irritation, and possibly burnout of both the mail clerk and the manager.

Consider this improved Tell:

Bob, I've got to talk to you about the mail. I've gotten some complaints about mail being delivered late. Yesterday two people said they didn't get the morning mail until after 2 in the afternoon. Optimally, all the morning mail should be sorted and ready for delivery by 11:30 and by 11:45 at the latest, and between 3:30 and 3:45 in the afternoon.

This improved Tell communicates expectations and lays the foundation for negotiations.

ASK

A stands for Ask. Here the manager places the problem in the lap of the performer who is the only one who can improve performance. Most people have at least some idea about what is stopping their performance and how to remove the block. The manager should avoid thinking of a solution but, instead, guide performers in developing their own solutions. This approach allows performers more responsibility and more personal power. Instead of being a disciplinarian, the manager is teacher, facilitator, and coach.

THE ASK STEP ELICITS PARTICIPATION.

The Ask step is vitally important and one that many managers tend to skip. Ask is where the participation of the performer is engaged. Ask for information about the problem and for suggestions on how to improve performance.

Use Open-Ended Questions

Use open-ended questions to prompt a response. These should begin with "What," "When," "Where," "Who," "How," and "In what way." Avoid questions that begin with "Why" because why questions tend to put people on the defensive. You may have to ask a couple of times, especially when first using TASC Plus.

Continue asking questions until you've gotten all relevant information. Remember, you can't ask too many questions. A manager never looks foolish asking questions.

Avoid Leading Questions

Avoid asking leading questions or questions that imply the answer you're seeking. It's a waste of time if the performer only tells you what he or she thinks you want to hear. Likewise, closed questions that elicit a yes/no answer are less effective. Closed questions such as "Do you...?" or "Are you...?" or "Can you...?" can feel like an interrogation.

Make sure to keep an open mind. There's no point in asking for suggestions if you've already predetermined what the problem is and what is going to be done. As soon as the employees pick up on the fact that you're not really listening to suggestions, they will clam up. Pay attention to what the person is saying. Encourage him or her to talk. Genuine interest will go a long way.

Ask for Information and Suggestions

The person in the job is the person who is closest to the particular work. This person knows, more than anyone else, problems that impact upon getting the job done. And this person probably has a number of good ideas for improving the way that his or her job is performed. When you tap into this wellspring of ideas, you simultaneously empower the employee. It gives people the feeling that they are important and that their input is needed.

Ask the employees for information and suggestions.

"Joe, what are your ideas about using positive feedback as a motivator?"

"Bob, what suggestions do you have for getting the morning mail out by 11:45?"

When performance is below the standard, ask what can be done to bring performance up to the standard.

"Shirley, your average defect rate is 12 percent above the standard. What suggestions do you have for getting those defects down?"

This communicates a concern with Shirley's performance without being critical or blaming. Again, the employee knows more about impediments to quality performance in his or her job than anyone else and probably has some good suggestions for solutions. Tap into this resource. By asking, you enlist participation.

Make sure that you listen to what is suggested.

If you ask and don't listen or dismiss what the employees say without careful consideration, you risk engendering a sense of futility.

When performance is above the standard, ask what will help keep performance at that high level.

"John, the accuracy of your cuts are exceptionally good. What can I do to help you stay at this high level?"

Set an Objective

S stands for Set Objective. When manager and performer have clarified what is impeding performance and what actions might facilitate it, they move to the objective-setting stage, where a short-term goal is determined. The suggestions made during the Ask step are a natural springboard for setting a short-term objective aimed at achieving or surpassing the standard. What precisely will the performer do?

THE EMPLOYEE SHOULD
SET THE OBJECTIVE

Once again, it's important to get the performer to set the objective. The manager should not set the objective but guide the performer, by asking questions, in doing so. The Set step is a means of teaching the worker to self-manage and self-motivate. In the early stages, the manager may have to take a more active role and teach the performer how to set objectives. Over time, however the individual in the job should become more active.

Take Small Steps

No objective is too small as long as it represents movement forward. A series of successful small steps is more effective than an objective that requires too much too soon, resulting in failure.

Be Specific

Once again, the objective should be very specific. A good objective specifies who will do what under which conditions (when and where) for how long. For example, Joe replied that he had learned from his father that a "swift kick" was the best motivator. He agreed, however, that a positive approach might work better than threats; but he didn't know how to start. In such a situation the manager might negotiate a small-step objective.

Joe, for the next week (how long), you're (who) going to pat each of your people on the back at least once a week (how much) by commenting on something he or she has done right (what). I'll come by this time next week to talk about how it worked out.

One Thing at a Time

Work on one behavior at a time. If there are two proposed actions, set two different objectives. It helps to write the objectives down. This emphasizes the importance and promotes clarity. Determine here how the behavior or outcome specified in the objective will be counted.

CHECK

C is for Check. Periodically check how the employee is doing. After an objective has been set the manager's role becomes one of facilitating and monitoring progress toward accomplishing that objective.

When possible have the employee track his or her own performance on a chart or graph. An employee can record the length of calls, times to do certain tasks, how many items completed, and so forth. Then when you, as manager, check on the employee you can look over the chart, which provides you with information about performance. Make sure to give the employee "wins" for keeping such performance records.

An additional advantage of the employee recording data on performance is that what one pays attention to tends to change in the desired direction. Thus, if employees keep track of the length of calls, and the objective is to shorten call length, simply keeping this information will tend to have a beneficial impact upon performance.

Acknowledge

Plus stands for acknowledging progress toward the objective. The rule of thumb is to look for and acknowledge what the person has done right, which I call "on-TASC performance". On-TASC performance is any action that contributes to achieving the objective. This includes gathering the data itself.

Suppose for example, the mail clerk collects data on the time that mail leaves the mail room and the number of letters returned as mismailed. Consider the following situations:

If the mail went out early and the number of returns is down, the manager should acknowledge the fact that mail went out early and that returns are down.

Bob, I see you got the mail out early today and that returns are down. Whatever you're doing to improve both of these seems to be working. This is great and I appreciate the extra effort that you've made to accomplish this. If there's anything I can do to help you keep this up, let me know.

If the mail went out on time but the number of returns exceeds the standard, the manager should acknowledge that mail went out on time and use TASC Plus to work on the returns.

Bob, I see that you've been getting the mail out every day on time. This is good. Let me know if there's anything I can do to assist you in keeping on schedule. I noticed that the number of returns is up to 37. As we discussed before you should keep returns to 20 or fewer per delivery (Tell). What suggestions do you have for cutting down on the number of returns (Ask)?

If mail went out later than usual and the number of returns is up but they are both still within the acceptable range, the manager would say nothing about mail time or returns but should acknowledge that the person recorded the data. In this case, recording data is the on-TASC behavior.

Bob, I appreciate the efforts you have made keeping track of information like this. You've done a good job by being thorough in keeping the data charts and this is important. It helps me do my job better.

A second rule of thumb is all drops in performance should be simply ignored except when it goes below the standard. In this case, the manager should avoid criticism or threats and recycle through TASC Plus.

BENEFITS OF TASC PLUS

By following TASC Plus, managers can prompt participation as well as gave feedback and reinforcement. Substandard performance need not be criticized; instead, it can be used as an opportunity to use TASC Plus to motivate by eliciting participation in solving the problem and focusing on constructive solutions. As a secondary gain, managers who use TASC Plus experience an increase in their own sense of controllability because they gain a feeling of "I can do."

The TASC Plus approach allows employees to maximize their personal power and harness that power in the service of organizational goals. It provides managers with a road map of what to do and how to do it. In the process the manager's role is transformed into that of teacher. Employees learn to set task goals and to participate in goal-setting for their own jobs and often in the definition and direction of the job itself. All organizations and the people in them are continually changing. TASC Plus provides a mechanism for on going change. Through the negotiation process expectations and directions can be modified and shaped in response to the demands of the organization and the needs of the individual. TASC Plus provides an objective basis for raises, promotions, and other organizational acknowledgement. And it takes the yearly performance review out of the manager's office and into the daily work routine. Expectations on all sides are clarified and people know how they are evaluated and what those evaluations are. Most important, TASC Plus maximizes individual responsibility and dignity.

It isn't necessary to make a big deal out of TASC Plus by calling the person in for a formal meeting. The interaction can take place informally right at the person's workstation. TASC Plus frees the manager to attend to other matters. He or she needs to occasionally check in on the performer, look at the data, and acknowledge on-TASC behavior. When workers get immediate feedback on their efforts to meet the objective they gain a sense of accomplishment for good performance and make immediate adjustments to stop problems.

TASC–Plus can be used in the normal flow of the work day.

TASC Plus is an effective management tool that helps the manager to keep a thumb on the pulse of the department, to identify problems, and to take corrective actions before they get out of control. It can provide a framework for a skilled manager to assist employees in making changes in their unproductive behaviors. At the setting-objective stage, for example, managers can guide employees through self-development programs. Effective coaching and other pertinent management skills and techniques are outlined in my book, Getting Peak Performance Every day: How to Manage Like a Coach.

Bibliography

Bandura, Albert. *Principles of Behavior Modification*, Holt, Rinehart and Winston, New York: 1969.

Bennett, Hal Zina and Susan J. Sparrow. *Follow Your Bliss*, Avon Books, New York: 1990.

Bennett, Steven J. *Playing Hardball with Soft Skills: How to Prosper with Non-Technical Skills in a High-Tech World*, Bantam, New York: 1986.

Boe, Anne and Bettie B. Youngs? *Is Your "Net" Working?*, John Wiley, New York: 1989.

Bolles, Richard N. *What Color Is Your Parachute?*, Ten Speed Press, Berkeley, CA: 1978.

Bower, Sharon A. and Gordon Bower. *Asserting Yourself: A Practical Guide To Positive Change*, Addison-Wesley, Reading, MA: 1976.

Brief, Arthur P., Randall S. Schuler, and Mary Van Sell. *Managing Job Stress*, Little Brown, Boston: 1981.

Brothers, Joyce. "All I Wanted Was A Cadillac," in *How to Get Whatever You Want Out of Life*, Simon and Schuster, New York: 1978, p.11-18.

Brown, Barbara. *Supermind: The Ultimate Energy*, Harper & Row, New York: 1980.

Browne, Harry. *How I Found Freedom In an Unfree World*, Avon, New York: 1973.

Brunton, Paul. *The Secret Path*, Dutton, New York: 1935.

Butler, Pamela. *Talking to Yourself: Learning the Language of Self-Support*, Harper & Row, New York: 1981.

Castaneda, Carlos. *The Teachings of Don Juan*, Pocket, New York: 1968.

Castaneda, Carlos. *The Second Ring of Power*, Simon and Schuster, New York: 1977.

Charland, Jr., William A. *Career Shifting: Starting Over In a Changing Economy*, Bob Adams, Inc. Publishers, Holbrook, MA: 1993.

Chin-Lee, Cynthia. *It's Who You Know: Career Strategies for Making Effective Personal Contacts*, Pfeiffer & Company, San Diego, CA: 1993.

Coffee, Gerald. *Beyond Survival: A POW's Inspiring Lesson in Living*, Berkley Books, New York: 1990.

Colligan, Douglas. "The High Priest of Guerrilla Psych," *Omni*, March 1980, pp. 108 - 115.

Connellan, Thomas. *How to Improve Human Performance: Behaviorism in Business and Industry*, Harper & Row, New York: 1978.

Coulter, Jr., N. Arthur. *Synergetics, An Adventure in Human Development*, Prentice-Hall, Englewood Cliffs, NJ: 1976.

Covey, Stephen R. *The 7 Habits of Highly Effective People: Powerful Lessons In Personal Change*, A Firestone Book, New York: 1989.

Csikszentmihalyi, Mihaly. *Flow: The Psychology of Optimal Experience,* Harper & Row, New York: 1990.

Deal, Terrence and Allen A. Kennedy. *Corporate Cultures: The Rites and Rituals of Corporate Life,* Addison Wesley, Reading, MA: 1982.

De Ropp, Robert. *The Master Game: Beyond the Drug Experience,* Delta, New York: 1968

Doore, Gary, Editor. *Shaman's Path: Healing, Personal Growth and Empowerment,* Shambhala, Boston: 1988.

Dyer, Wayne. *Pulling Your Own Strings,* Thomas Y. Crowell Co., New York: 1978.

Dyer, Wayne. *The Sky's the Limit,* Pocket Books, New York: 1980.

Ellis, Albert and Robert A. Harper. *A New Guide to Rational Living,* Wilshire Books, North Hollywood, CA: 1979.

"The Essential Hangout," *Psychology Today,* April, 1980. pp. 82.

Fields, Rick, with Peggy Taylor, Rex Weyler, and Rick Ingrasci. *Chop Wood, Carry Water: A Guide to Finding Spiritual Fulfillment in Everyday Life,* Tarcher, Los Angeles: 1984.

Freudenberger, Herbert J. *Burnout: The High Cost of High Achievement,* Anchor/ Doubleday, New York: 1980.

Gallwey, Timothy and Bob Kriegel. *Inner Skiing,* Random House, New York: 1977.

Garfield, Charles. *Peak Performers: The New Heroes of American Business,* Avon: New York: 1986.

Gilbert, Thomas F. *Human Competence: Engineering Worthy Performance,* McGraw Hill, New York: 1978.

Gupton, Ted and Michael D. LeBow. "Behavior Management in a Large Industrial Firm," *Behavior Therapy,* Vol. 2. 1971, pp. 78 - 82.

Haga, William James, and Nichlos Acocella. *Haga's Law: Why Nothing Works and No One Can Fix It and the More We Try the Worse It Gets,* Morrow, New York: 1980.

Irish, Richard. *Go Hire Yourself an Employer,* Anchor Books, 1978.

Jaffe, Dennis. *Working With the Ones You Love,* Conari Press, Berkeley, CA: 1990.

Jaffee, Dennis T., and Cynthia Scott. *From Burnout to Balance: A Workbook for Peak Performance and Self-Renewal,* McGraw-Hill, New York: 1984.

Jaffee, Dennis T., and Cynthia Scott. *Take This Job and Love It: How to Change Your Work Without Changing Your Job,* Simon & Schuster, New York: 1988.

Janis, Irving L. and Leon Mann. *Decision Making: A Psychological Analysis of Conflict, Choice, and Commitment,* The Free Press, New York: 1977.

John-Roger and Peter McWilliams. *DO IT! Let's Get Off Our Butts: A Guide To Living Your Dreams,* Prelude Press, Los Angeles: 1991.

Kahn, Robert, Donald Wolf, Robert Quinn and Diedrick Snack. *Organizational Stress: Studies in Role Conflict and Ambiguity,* Wiley, New York: 1964.

Kennedy, Marilyn Moats. *Career Knockouts: How to Battle Back,* Warner Books, New York: 1980.

Keyes, Ken. *Handbook to Higher Consciousness,* Living Love Publications, Coos Bay, OR: 1978.

Keyes, Ken and Bruce Burkan. *How To Make Your Life Work or Why Aren't You Happy?,* Cornerstone Library, New York: 1976.

Lakoff, George and Mark Johnson. *Metaphors We Live By*, University of Chicago Press, Chicago: 1980.

Lazarus, Arnold. *In the Mind's Eye: The Power of Imagery Therapy to Give You Control Over Your Life*, Hawson, New York: 1977.

Lefkowitz, Bernard. *Breaktime: Living Without Work in a Nine-To-Five World*, Penguin Books, New York: 1979.

Leiter, Michael P., and Christina Maslach. *Banish Burnout: Six Strategies for Improving Your Relationship with Work*, Jossey-Bass, San Francisco, CA., 2005.

Leiter, Michael P., *Preventing Burnout and Building Engagement*, Jossey-Bass, San Francisco, CA 2000.

Leonard, George. *Mastery: The Keys To Success and Long-Term Fulfillment*, New American Library, New York: 1991.

LeShan, Lawrence. *How to Meditate*, Bantam Books, New York: 1974.

Lewinson, Peter, Ricardo Munoz, Mary Ann Youngren, and Antonette Zeiss. *Control Your Depression*, Prentice-Hall, Englewood Cliffs, NJ: 1978.

Marks, Linda. *Living With Vision*, Knowledge Systems, Indianapolis: 1989.

Maslach, Christina. "Burned-Out," *Human Behavior*, September 1976, p. 16.

Maslach, Christina. *The Truth About Burnout: How Organizations Cause Personal Stress and What to Do About It*, Jossey-Bass, San Francisco, CA 1997.

Mason, L. John. *Guide To Stress Reduction*, Celestial Arts, Berkeley, CA: 1985.

Medley, H. Anthony. *Sweaty Palms: The Neglected Art of Being Interviewed*, Lifetime Learning Publications, Belmont, CA: 1978.

Mehrabian, Albert. *Public Places and Private Spaces: The Psychology of Work, Play and Living Environments*, New York: Basic Books, 1976.

Miller, Emmett E. and Deborah Lueth. *Feeling Good: How to Stay Healthy*, Prentice-Hall, Englewood Cliffs, NJ:1978.

Miller, Lyle H., and Alma Dell Smith. *The Stress Solution: An Action Plan To Manage The Stress In Your Life*, Pocket Books, New York: 1993.

Moreau, Daniel. *Take Charge of Your Career: How to Survive and Profit from a Mid-Career Change*, Kiplinger Books, Washington D.C. : 1990.

Morehouse, Laurence E. and Leonard Gross. *Maximum Performance*, Pocket Books, New York: 1978.

Nair, Keshavan. *Beyond Winning: The Handbook For The Leadership Revolution*, Paradox Press, Phoenix: 1990.

Ostrander, Sheila, Lynn Schroeder and Nancy Ostrander. *Super-learning*, Delacorte Press, New York: 1979.

Pearce, Joseph Chilton. *The Crack in the Cosmic Egg: Challenging Constructs of Mind and Reality*, Pocket Books, New York: 1971.

Potter, Beverly A. *Get Peak Performance Every Day: How to Manage Like a Coach*, Ronin Punlishing, Berkeley, CA, 2004.

Potter, Beverly A., *High Performance Goal Setting: Using Intuition to Conceive and Achieve Your Dreams*, Ronin Publishing, Berkeley, CA, 1999.

Potter, Beverly A. "Managing Authority: How to Give Directives" in *Turning Around: Keys to Motivation and Productivity*, Ronin Publishing, Berkeley, CA: 1987.

Potter, Beverly A. *Preventing Job Burnout*, Crisp Publications, Menlo Park, CA: 1996.

Potter, Beverly A. "Self-Management" in *Turning Around: Keys to Motivation and*

Productivity, Ronin Publishing, Berkeley, CA: 1987.

Potter, Beverly A. *The Way of the Ronin: Riding the Waves of Change at Work*, Ronin Publishing, Berkeley, CA: 2001.

Potter, Beverly A., *Worrywarts Companion: Twenty-One Ways to Soothe Yourself and Worry Smart*, Wild Cat canyon Press, Berkeley, Ca 1996.

Reps, Paul, editor. *Zen Flesh, Zen Bones: A Collection of Zen and Pre-Zen writings*, Doubleday, New York.

Rosen, Gerald. *The Relaxation Book*, Prentice Hall, Englewood Cliffs, NJ: 1977.

Scheele, Adele M. *Skills For Success: A Guide to the Top*, Morrow, New York: 1980.

Schumacher, E. F., and Peter N. Gillingham. *Good Work*, Harper & Row, New York:1979.

Seligman, Martin E. P. *Helplessness: On Depression, Development, and Death*, W. H. Freeman & Co., San Francisco: 1975.

Simon, Sidney B. *Getting Unstuck: Breaking Through Your Barriers to Change*, Warner Books, New York: 1988.

Sinetar, Marsha. *Do What You Love, The Money Will Follow: Discovering Your Right Livelihood*, Paulist Press, New York: 1987.

Shah, Idries. *Tales of the Dervishes*, New York: Dutton, 1970.

Shapiro, Dean H. Jr. *Precision Nirvana*, Spectrum Books, Englewood Cliffs, NJ: 1978.

Sheehy, Gail. *Passages: Predictable Crisis Of Adult Life*, Bantam, New York: 1976.

Sher, Barabra. *Wishcraft: How To Get What You Really Want*, Ballantine, New York: 1979.

Silva, Jose, and Philip Miele. *The Silva Mind Control Method*, Simon & Schuster, New York:1977.

Smith, Manuel. *Kicking The Fear Habit*, The Dial Press, New York: 1977.

Stevens, Paul. *Stop Postponing The Rest of Your Life*, Ten Speed Press, Berkeley, CA: 1993.

Truch, Stephen. *Teacher Burnout and What to Do About It*, Academic Therapy Publications, Novato, CA: 1980.

Veninga, Robert L. and James P. Spradley. *The Work Stress Connection: How to Cope with Burnout*, Ballantine, New York: 1981.

Waitley, Denis and Reni L. Witt. *The Joy of Working: The 30-Day System to Success, Wealth, and Happiness on the Job*, Ballantine, New York: 1985.

Wassmer, Arthur, C. *Making Contact: A Guide To Overcoming Shyness, Making New Relationships and Keeping Those You Already Have*, The Dial Press, New York:1978.

Watson, David L. and Roland G. Tharp. *Self-Directed Behavior: Self-Modification for Personal Adjustment*, Brooks/Gale, Monterey, CA: 1972.

West, Ross. *How to Be Happier in the Job You Sometimes Can't Stand*, Boradman, Nashville: 1990.

Young, Jeffrey, E., and Janet S. Klosko. *Reinventing Your Life: How To Break Free From Negative Patterns*, Dutton, New York: 1993.

Zaleznick, Abraham, Manfred frets de Writs, and John Howards: "Stress Reactions in Organizations: Syndromes, Causes, and Consequences," *Behavioral Science* (Vol. 22), pg 77.

Zastrow, Charles. *Talk To Yourself Using the Power of Self-Talk*, Spectrum Books, Englewood Cliffs, NJ: 1979.

Index

Docpotter's Library

For useful career information,
visit Docpotter's website at docpotter.com.

RONIN BOOKS FOR INDEPENDENT MINDS

PREVENTING JOB BURNOUT ....Potter PREJOB 12.95 ___
  Workbook: How to renew enthusiasm for work.

HIGH PERFORMANCE GOAL SETTING ....Potter HIGOAL 9.95 ___
  How to use intuition to conceive and achieve your dreams.

GET PEAK PERFORMANCE EVERY DAY ....Potter GETPEA 12.95 ___
  How to manage like a coach.

FINDING A PATH WITH A HEART .... Potter FINPAT 14..95 ___
  How to go from burnout to bliss, principles of self-leading.

THE WAY OF THE RONIN ....Potter WAYRON 14.95 ___
  Maverick career strategies for riding the waves of change at work.

FROM CONFLICT TO COOPERATION ....Potter FROCON 14.95 ___
  How to mediate a dispute, step-by-step technique.

MAVERICK AS MASTER IN THE MARKET PLACE ....Potter MAVMAS 9.95 ___
  Audio: The way of the office warrior

WORRYWART'S COMPANION ....Potter WORWAR 12.95 ___
  21 ways to soothe yourself and worry smart.

DRUG TESTING AT WORK ....Potter & Orfali DRUTES 24.95 ___
  A guide for employers.

PASS THE TEST ....Potter & Orfali PASTES 16.95 ___
  An employee guide to drug testing.

                              Books prices: SUBTOTAL $_____

                    CA customers add sales tax 8.75% _____
                              BASIC SHIPPING: (All orders) $5.00
  PLUS SHIPPING: USA+$1 for each book, Canada+$2 for each book
                    Europe+$7 for each book, Pacific+$10 for each book $_____
                              Books + Tax + Basic + Shipping: TOTAL $_____
Checks payable to **Ronin Publishing**

MC _ Visa _ Exp date _ _ - _ _ card #: _ _ _ _ _ _ _ _ _ _ _ _ _ _ _ _ (sign) _ _ _ _ _ _ _ _ _

Name_ _

_

Address _ City _ _ _ _ _ _ _ _ _ _ _ _ State _ _ _ ZIP _ _ _ _

_

☞ Call for our FREE catalog. On-line catalog-> www.roninpub.com

Ⓒ **Orders (800)858-2665 • Info (510)420-3669 • Fax (510)420-3672**
  Available at amazon.com or order through your independent book-